Tips for Success

Guide for Instrumental Music Teachers

Secrets revealed from teaching legends and leading music educators that will help make your job easier—these proven success strategies can help provide solutions for some of those everyday challenges we all face in education. The Music Achievement Council has consolidated and indexed these ideas into an easy-to-use format that is sure to become a quick reference guide that you will use regularly.

Produced by the Music Achievement Council

The **Music Achievement Council (MAC)** is an action-oriented nonprofit organization sponsored by the National Association of School Music Dealers (NASMD) and the National Association of Music Merchants (NAMM). MAC is made up of three representatives from NASMD, three manufacturers and suppliers of Instrumental Music products and one representative from NAMM. The group's purpose is to promote instrumental music participation with particular emphasis on producing materials that encourage and motivate students to join—and stay in—band and orchestra. The council was formed in 1983 and reorganized in 1990, forming a nonprofit 501(c)(3) organization.

The Music Achievement Council appreciates the support and guidance of NAMM in the development of these materials.

Focusing on the Classroom:
A Checklist for Teachers

What does a music teacher do? They teach classes, share their love of music with students, prepare lesson plans, develop curriculum, assess and evaluate students' progress, and share this information with parents, fellow teachers and school administrators.

The following are some ideas to help you become the best professional music educator you can, as well as realize the full potential in each of your students.

Noteworthy Concepts to Keep in Mind as You Start Your Career:

- **Be genuine.** Students can spot insincerity.
- **Be enthusiastic.** Enthusiasm is contagious and will help prevent discipline problems. Students will enjoy your class and remain on task if they are engaged and enjoy what they are doing. You need to get the students on your side. If they see that **YOU** are sold on your product—music education—[it is infectious] they will be inspired by your passion.
- **Keep things moving!** Plan a well-paced lesson with lots of variety.
- **Be fair to all students.** Be very careful that you do not choose "favorites." This takes constant vigilance because you naturally like some students better than others. Look for a good quality in each student and capitalize on it.
- **Take an interest in what the students are doing outside of your classroom.** The students will respond to you even more if they know you are genuinely interested in them.
- **Be professional.** Value the time of your students, parents, colleagues and administrators. Have high expectations of yourself and maintain consistency in all that you do.
- **Communicate clearly and often.** State procedures and expectations in writing and share them with students, parents and staff as early in the year as possible. Provide reminders regularly and follow up individual concerns with a phone call.
- **Praise in public, discipline in private.** Avoid confrontations with students in front of the class. Students will do anything to save face in front of their peers, and confrontations denigrate teacher authority. Above all, never "lose it" in front of your class.
- **Ask for help.** The best teachers ask for help when things are not going perfectly. Discuss problems with those who can help to resolve them and remember that the job of a supervisor is to help you.
- **Be a good listener.** When others communicate with you, give them your undivided attention. This shows that you care and are truly interested.

- **Communicate with other new teachers.** You will discover that most new teachers are experiencing similar problems and you may be able to help each other solve them.

- **Develop a support network.** Colleagues of all ages and experience levels, former teachers and professional organizations—the profession is filled with individuals who are eager to share their time to help ensure your success.

- **Develop your own teaching style.** Use what works best for you. Work **with** your personality, not **against** it.

- **Build students' confidence.** Students will become self-confident when they know they can trust you.

- **Be consistent, yet flexible.** Do not vary expectations and format greatly, yet keep in mind that each student is different.

- **Expect students to respect others and model that behavior consistently.** Correct inappropriate behavior promptly and fairly.

- **Be prepared for *every* lesson.** Make a plan and stick to it. Think of your plan as a checklist of things to accomplish within a given time, and teach every class to the top of your game. ***Never teach "by the seat of your pants."***

- **Write down all contest and festival deadlines on a calendar.** Make sure you meet deadlines early. Many entries are by postmark deadline and you can't always be sure the envelope or package is postmarked the day it is mailed.

- **Always be on the lookout for new music. Visit local music stores; attend conferences, conventions and concerts in your search for new music.** Mark up programs and keep them in a separate file so that you are always ready to order should funds suddenly become available (this occurs frequently toward the end of the year when fiscal budgets have to be expended).

- **Select music for the students that they will learn from and enjoy.** As the students become more informed consumers of music, they will value a wider variety of literature.

- **Order extra scores for solos or parts in advance for future concerts and festivals.** Publishers get thousands of requests at the same time of the year.

- **Keep an accurate inventory of all instruments and uniforms.** This is necessary for insurance purposes and will help you design a replacement plan.

- **Review mailings that come from manufacturers and publishers.** These are designed to help you be successful. Plan to use interesting teaching and performing materials—and stay out of ruts. Challenge yourself!

- **Don't be afraid to promote your program, but do not do it at the expense of anyone else.** You should not start an "us-against-them" attitude.

- **Stay informed.** Join your state and national professional organization, and an arts-education advocacy group. Knowing what is happening on a state and national level will enable you to improve your local environment for arts education.

- **Stay current.** Professional development is critical to your success. Visit outstanding programs. Incorporate successful techniques you observe in your teaching. Share what you learn with your colleagues.

- **Enjoy yourself.** Don't take yourself too seriously. Humor is an important teaching tool.

- **Do your best. Nothing more can be asked.**

MOST IMPORTANTLY, make sure the students know you care. Students will not care what you know until they know that you care. As a wise student teaching supervisor once said, "You've got to love the kids."

Want more tips for keeping music strong in your schools?
Visit the site devoted to all things music advocacy: **www.supportmusic.com**

Tips for Success is produced by the Music Achievement Council • www.musicachievementcouncil.org • 800.767.6266

Focusing on the Classroom:
Music Content Standards

The **National Standards for Arts Education** constitute one of the **biggest educational reform** efforts ever undertaken in American education. The standards focus on where the action is—at the local level, the grassroots level. The National Standards aren't prescriptive because **community control of local schools is a guiding principle** in American education. Community control, however, also means community responsibility. The **arts standards do set important targets** for a student's **academic knowledge and achievement** in music, dance, theatre and visual arts, as measured at the end of grades 4, 8 and 12. They give our communities the benchmarks we need to fulfill our **responsibility to our students.**

What are the National Music Content Standards?

- Singing, alone and with others, a varied repertoire of music
- Performing on instruments, alone and with others, a varied repertoire of music
- Improvising melodies, variations and accompaniments
- Composing and arranging music within specified guidelines
- Reading and notating music
- Listening to, analyzing and describing music
- Evaluating music and musical performances
- Understanding relationships between music, the other arts and disciplines outside the arts
- Understanding music in relation to history and culture

Implementing Standards

Excerpted from a presentation given by Paul R. Lehman, for the Iowa Alliance for Arts Education.

National, voluntary standards have been developed for music, visual arts, theatre and dance. Nearly every school in the nation offers instruction in music and the visual arts. Programs in theater and dance tend to be less widespread and less fully developed. Although we seek full implementation of the standards in all four disciplines, we recognize that different schedules for implementation in the four disciplines may be necessary. If you support arts education, you are urged to do these things:

- **Get to know the other arts educators in the schools in your community.** Find out if there is a balanced, comprehensive and sequential program in each of the arts offered in the schools.
- **Encourage the arts educators** in the schools of your community to adapt their programs to reflect the national standards.

TIP 2

- **Get to know** the principals, superintendent and other school officials in your community. Make them aware of your support for strong arts programs.

- **Explain to everyone** who plays a role in education decision making why the arts should be a part of the curriculum for every American child. Emphasize that both the *Goals 2000: Educate America Act* and *Prisoners of Time*, the report of the National Education Commission on Time and Learning, include the arts among the basics of the curriculum.

- **As standards in the various disciplines are released** and considered for adoption, point out to education decision makers that we now have national standards for arts education as well. Lobby for the adoption of the national standards for arts education at the state and local levels, and push as hard as possible for implementation.

- **When the arts standards cannot be fully implemented** immediately, encourage the development of an incremental plan for implementing the standards in each of the arts as completely and as rapidly as possible.

- **Whenever a newspaper columnist** or editorial writer suggests that the arts are not high priority or that we can get along without arts programs in our schools, write a well-reasoned but firm letter opposing that viewpoint. Let no negative opinion pass unchallenged, regardless of where you live.

- **Encourage business leaders** to support arts programs in the schools. Apart from the value of the arts for their own sake to all Americans, major corporations recognize the importance of education in the arts for their employees, and research shows that the economic impact of the arts at the state and local levels is enormous.

- Lobby for the appointment of a supervisor or coordinator in each of the arts if these positions do not already exist in your school district. The positions are necessary to provide leadership for each program and to ensure coordination, articulation and balance in the curriculum.

- Do not be satisfied with a program in the elementary schools in which the arts, especially music and the visual arts, are taught entirely by classroom teachers without the help of specialists. Very few classroom teachers can do an acceptable job alone. If classroom teachers are expected to play a major role, seek to ensure that the ability to teach at least two of the arts is a condition of employment.

- Do not be satisfied with a program that relies excessively on artists-in-residence or other enrichment activities. Exposure and enrichment are invaluable as supplements but are not substitutes for a balanced, comprehensive and sequential program in each of the arts in the curriculum. Make sure parents and administration are aware of the differences.

- Use your influence to ensure that the state of improvement plan being developed in your state guarantees a place for the arts.

- Encourage others to support the arts in the schools. If your friends and co-workers will recruit their friends on behalf of the arts, and they will recruit theirs, the number of supporters of arts education will eventually become overwhelming.

- Help to organize in-service education opportunities to help educators who may not be comfortable with some of the expectations of the standards.

- **Help to make education decision makers** and the public aware of what students are learning in the arts programs in your community. After a band parents' open house, one parent said, "I didn't know the kids actually learned things in band. I thought they just played." The same comment is often made about the visual arts, theater and dance. Don't let that happen in your community.

- **Work with the professional arts** education associations to monitor continuously everything that goes on in your state capitol with respect to education reform to ensure that the arts are treated fairly.

Arts Education Assessment

In September 1993, the Council of Chief State School Officers (CCSSO) convened a consortium of states interested in developing large-scale, state-level assessments in arts education. The State Collaborative on Assessments and Student Standards (SCASS) Arts Education Project developed and refined arts-education assessment instruments (classroom, large-scale and portfolio) that address the voluntary National Standards for Arts Education. The consortium conducted a professional development survey in 15 member states and field-tested the assessment exercise sets with 3,400 students in 76 schools.

Want more tips for keeping music strong in your schools?
Visit the site devoted to all things music advocacy: **www.supportmusic.com**

TIP 2

Tips for Success is produced by the Music Achievement Council • www.musicachievementcouncil.org • 800.767.6266

Focusing on the Classroom:
Know the Territory

What You Should Know about the Music Programs in Your Area

Survey the directors in surrounding and/or similar school districts to obtain the information below. The information will be helpful as you work to build your program's resources. Photocopy this sheet so you have a record of each district's response.

District Surveyed: **Date:**

District Level

- Y/N   Has a music coordinator
- Y/N   Has written music curriculum
- Y/N   Funds music program through district budget
- Y/N   Updates books and equipment regularly
- Y/N   Provides equal access for all students to music program

Elementary Level

- Y/N   Has music-certified instructor
- Y/N   Offers band and orchestra programs
- Y/N   Provides 100 minutes of music instruction weekly
- Y/N   Teaches varied music types through varied activities
- Y/N   Students create music

Middle/Junior High Level

- Y/N   Offers band, orchestra and choral programs during regular school day
- Y/N   Provides six or more periods in the school day
- Y/N   Teaches varied music styles

High School Level

- Y/N   Has music-certified instructor
- Y/N   Requires fine arts credit for graduation
- Y/N   Offers band, orchestra and choral programs during regular school day
- Y/N   Offers credit for band, orchestra and choral classes
- Y/N   Includes the band, orchestra and choral grades in students' overall GPA
- Y/N   Offers non-performance music courses for credit during regular school day

Adapted from MENC Teacher's Guide for Advocacy

TIP 3

Want more tips for keeping music strong in your schools?
Visit the site devoted to all things music advocacy: **www.supportmusic.com**

Tips for Success is produced by the Music Achievement Council • www.musicachievementcouncil.org • 800.767.6266

Focusing on the Classroom:
Recruiting and Retaining Students

Quality in a music program is dependent on a high rate of returning students and a reliable feeder network. With many courses competing for the same students, recruiting enough students to keep instrumental and vocal programs healthy is essential. It is the educator's responsibility to sell students and their parents on the value of signing up for an elective course in music.

Taking Action through Positive Experiences

- Among the reasons offered by parents and youngsters for NOT participating in music are a failure to be told about the nature and benefits of ensemble participation; lack of information about costs and available instrument rental plans; and concern over the amount of time that must be devoted in order to participate successfully.

- Music educators are challenged to provide a program that can successfully compete with the many demands on student time both in and out of school. Additionally, many administrators and school boards base their budget decisions on student numbers. A static or declining enrollment may doom music departments to static or declining budgets, staff reductions and reduced course offerings. Recruiting and retaining as many students as possible is vital. Without recruiting, public school music could disappear. You play the crucial role in this ongoing process.

First Performance, ASAP

We can remember the excitement of our first performance: The dress requirement, being the center of attention but with the security of the group, the applause of the audience—these are all memories that last a lifetime. You will never have a more enthusiastic group of performers and audience members than beginning music students and their parents, and an initial concert early in their development can ensure a strong program with a great deal of support.

The objectives of First Performances are fourfold:

- To reduce your beginner drop-out rate

- To provide short-term incentive goals

- To encourage communications with parents

- To further strengthen administrative support of your program

The first concert should be presented between the second and third month of the school year and students should be ready to demonstrate the first five notes. On the first night of the rental program, announce the date. The concert should be approximately 20 minutes long and take place in an informal setting.

Tips for Success

TIP 4

The best "First Performances" have parents participate actively. This is a time to help parents understand the value of establishing good habits such as practicing with a good chair and music stand; encouraging regular practice with practice sheets; caring for the instrument; and breathing and bowing techniques.

To help organize the First Performance Concert, an action kit is available from the Music Achievement Council at www.musicachievementcouncil.org. The kit contains all of the concert support materials you will need, including:

- A sample letter to parents
- A sample letter to administrators
- A poster to announce the performance
- A program blank
- A complete 20-minute concert, which includes parts for all instruments (uses only five notes—concert B-flat to F in whole, half and quarter notes and rests)

All you need to supply is:

- Someone to serve as an announcer
- Programs to be handed out as souvenir copies
- Light refreshments are optional

District-wide Concerts

Most successful ensemble programs use a district-wide concert as a promotional activity to give their students, parents, administration and community an enjoyable overview of the music program. The objectives of this event are to:

- Showcase student achievements
- Create interest in music and music education
- Increase communication with parents, administration and the community
- Strengthen administrative support
- Improve recruiting and retention rates

An all-district concert is a great public relations tool because it provides the community with a "musical snapshot" of the sequence of instruction from elementary through high school. In 90 minutes, students and parents see firsthand how far they've come and where they are going.

Informances

Every performance should have an "informance" component. While you are exciting youngsters about music, you are informing the parents about the value of an education in music. Written materials that explain the value of music in improving student achievement and self-esteem should be shared with the audience. This can take the form of short statements or quotes, or full-page program inserts detailing the latest findings of reliable research. The selection introduced through the informance can be showcased at a future concert, thus giving insight into the "before" and "after" music education process. Consider including a rehearsal and/or sight-reading component as part of your concert so the audience can gain a better understanding of the ensemble development process.

Getting Them into the Program

Fifth grade is typically the year that students are provided with the first opportunity to participate in public school instrumental programs. Creating a desire to participate in the programs begins with third and fourth grade students. To enhance the recruiting process, ensemble teachers need to work in partnership with general music teachers and classroom teachers. Teachers should work with students by using recorders; invite potential students to concerts; perform concerts at the elementary school; and provide demonstrations for students in the lower grades. Young students will remember what they saw and heard. If it's good, they will want to be a part of it, so make these performances meaningful and age-appropriate.

Keeping Them in the Program

It is important to recruit effectively, but it is even more important to keep students in the music program. The Gemeinhardt Report identifies that the No. 1 reason students leave a music program is the fear of failure. Recruiting assemblies, joint concerts, parent meetings and activities to increase retention during the elementary/middle school and middle school/high school transitions are some of the ways to boost enrollment. Remember, "You can't push a rope. You can only pull it." The best way to guarantee that students will remain committed to the program is to provide inspirational leadership in an exciting musical experience.

*To learn more, you can visit **www.musicachievementcouncil.org** to order your copy of The Practical Guide to Recruiting and Retention, which has assisted educators in a variety of challenging environments to build and maintain successful music programs.*

Want more tips for keeping music strong in your schools?
Visit the site devoted to all things music advocacy: **www.supportmusic.com**

TIP 4

The Business Side of Teaching School Music:
Working with Administrators

Instrumental teachers have a keen interest in professional development—studying conducting, instructional techniques, ensemble development and literature. Despite this commitment to professional growth, the thrill of having an outstanding ensemble eludes many directors.

Music Administration

- Music administration is a craft in which there is generally more than one right solution to a problem. To develop a strategy that maximizes your efforts, it is important to work within the system to obtain the staff, equipment and help you need.

- The relationship you establish with the school principal will help (or hinder) every aspect of your program. The principal's decisions about staffing, scheduling, building procedures and budgets set the priorities for the entire school. It is essential to understand what is important to individual administrators. Listen carefully!

- Develop a supportive relationship with the school custodians, bus drivers, cafeteria staff, maintenance personnel and tech support staff.

- Be a part of the team and advance your leader's priorities whenever possible. Your program will soon become one of those priorities.

- Just as teachers set goals for students, it is important to know the goals that the principal has for the music program. These may include discipline procedures, scheduling, budgets, relationships with parents and the number of ensemble performances.

- Each principal is guided by district goals. Learn what these are and discuss how music fits into these district-wide goals.

- Know what criteria the administration will use to evaluate the music department. The best objectives are specific, measurable and musically understood. Remember, it is important for administrators to observe rehearsals. This is when you are at your best, managing a large group of students in a complex activity. The process of teaching music is the exciting part of the job. Be sure to get credit for it.

- It is equally important to let administrators know what is important to you, students and parents. In most school districts, teachers set goals for themselves; these become part of the evaluation process, so use this opportunity to put them in writing. Some of these expectations may include concert attendance, community service obligations, budgeting assistance, participation in awards ceremonies, letters to parents and scheduling. Consult administrators when developing ensemble policies rather than after sharing them with students.

TIP 5

- An administrator's scarcest resource is time. Value that time by being organized when you meet. Whenever possible, bring two or three recommended solutions or suggestions, not just problems, to meetings. Be proactive—suggest opportunities that benefit the students and the school.

- When making a proposal, include all the relevant information. In most cases, you will end up with what you negotiate.

- Never miss an opportunity to improve how the students and the music program are perceived by others in the building and community. Advocate for high standards and develop a reputation as a team player in your educational community.

- Always keep the best interests of your students first when making decisions. If you follow this tenet, you will rarely make a poor decision. If unsure, consult with your supervisor for guidance.

- Always follow through on commitments.

- Have solutions for problems before they occur.

- Avoid the divide-and-conquer approach.

- Never point to another program except to recognize excellence.

- Make time to visit with colleagues.

A Short Checklist for Building Valuable Relationships

- Show interest in the activities of others.

- Include the principal and other faculty members as special guest soloists or narrators on concerts.

- Help your principal prepare congratulatory letters to students selected for special honors. Everyone enjoys participating in a winning activity.

- If the band missed a day of school to attend a competition, thank the faculty for their support and accommodation.

- Keep faculty informed of department activities and concerts; send every member of the faculty a copy of the music department calendar.

- Regardless of age, have the music students send personal concert invitations to members of the administration, faculty and school board.

- Sign up to chaperone a dance, cover a math or science class, attend a basketball game and serve on committees.

- Share success! By helping others to be successful, you share in that success as well.

Want more tips for keeping music strong in your schools?
Visit the site devoted to all things music advocacy: **www.supportmusic.com**

TIP 5

Tips for Success is produced by the Music Achievement Council • www.musicachievementcouncil.org • 800.767.6266

The Business Side of Teaching School Music:
Choosing a Music Dealer

Instrumental music directors and parents should know that one of **the strongest supporters** of school music programs has been and continues to be **the local full-service, school-oriented music dealer**. Direct-mail and Internet retailers usually trade on price and do not offer service or in-depth concern for the local school programs or community.

A **working "partnership"** with a full-service dealer can **benefit your program and save time** in a variety of ways. Numerous services are almost always offered by the local dealer, but not necessarily by the out-of-state, telephone-based or Internet retailer.

You Should Expect:

- **The music dealer** to have an established reputation of honest, fair and successful dealings with school music programs. This reputation will have been established by the services and support previously provided to the school.

- **The dealer representatives** to understand the needs of your students and your music program.

- **The dealer representatives** to conduct themselves in a professional manner when dealing with faculty, administration, students and parents.

- **Regular personal service calls** scheduled on a consistent basis by their professional educational representatives.

- **A complete, in-house repair shop** with highly trained technicians to care for all student-owned and school-owned instruments, including double reeds. All work should be fully guaranteed and completed with minimum interruption to your program.

- **Competitive prices** for school bids.

- **Lease programs** for new instrument purchases.

- **Specially priced** folders, activity calendars and instrument name tags.

- **A comprehensive student-recruiting program** supported by dealer personnel in cooperation with the school staff and administration.

The Music Dealer Should:

- Be an **authorized selling agent** for a wide variety of instrument brands.

- **Provide loaner instruments** for repair needs.

- **Make available a broad selection** of method books, and ensemble and solo literature.

- **Provide advocacy materials** and educational research reports for your use.

TIP 6

And Remember. . .

- **Your local dealer maintains a substantial** inventory of instruments, accessories and printed music in anticipation of your classroom and ensemble needs. When you need services on instruments and equipment found in your band and orchestra rooms, your local school music dealer is there for you.

- Local dealers are often former band directors who **understand the school music program** and are committed to serving the needs and total health of your music program.

- These services are provided to help you be a successful music educator. **Support those who support you!**

A Sound Recruiting Program:

- **Written music aptitude tests** given to all eligible classes to appraise natural ability

- **Provide and show** a music motivation and recruiting film

- **Pre-test all interested students** to assure physical capability on the instrument of their choice and/or help guide them in making their choice

Your Music Dealer Can Help!

- **Provide—free of charge—**high-quality instruments for the purposes of testing the students

- **Provide band-recruiting posters** for in-school use

- **Convenient in-school availability** of rental instruments, books and music stands

- **Trained music personnel** to talk with parents and offer guidance if requested

- **Pre-checking** each instrument that is rented or leased to ensure it is in top playing condition

- **Equip each instrument** that is rented or leased with the necessary accessories for the beginner to get started (for example: reeds, cork grease, oils and swabs)

Want more tips for keeping music strong in your schools?
Visit the site devoted to all things music advocacy: **www.supportmusic.com**

TIP 6

Tips for Success is produced by the Music Achievement Council • www.musicachievementcouncil.org • 800.767.6266

The Business Side of Teaching School Music:
Fiscal Procedures

Each school district has **specific procedures** that directors follow in order to conduct business. The best time to check on these procedures is during your job interview. **Review these procedures** with your administration once you have started your new job.

Know what your administrators expect and follow their directions to minimize errors that can cost your district time and money, as well as a delayed payment to your vendor.

Work with Appropriate Personnel

- Depending on the procedures in your building or school district, you will work with any number of staff when making purchases. The most important thing to remember is that **there are ALWAYS policies involved when spending taxpayer dollars**. Do not place orders without receiving instructions on how to do so beforehand. Not following procedures with regard to district funds can lead to dismissal.

- **Recognize the importance** of the functions performed by your district regarding the reporting of the financial information of the school district in accordance with district policies and procedures and state and federal laws and regulations.

1. Know the state laws regarding purchasing for public entities such as a school district.

- In some locales, **purchases of items in excess** of a certain amount are required to be bid. **Bidding** usually requires additional time—drawing up specifications that are best suited to your program's needs, as well as the time needed to request, receive, tabulate and award bids.

- Find out **how many bids** must be received.

- **Be specific** with the item descriptions given to the companies from which you are requesting bids. Mention brands, models, delivery time, delivery charges, etc.

- **Confirm** the company is a reputable dealer for the items you need.

- **Reconfirm** the company can and will provide service after the purchase if warranty work is needed.

- Keep in mind that school bids are usually done with a **minimal profit margin.** Most music dealers prepare school bids as a **service to their customers.** Paying less for an item only to have service problems later is probably not worth the savings gained. Cheaper is not always less expensive.

- **Consider doing business locally** to assure that instruments are properly serviced and maintained in a timely and cost-effective manner. Purchasing locally also means the money and taxes stay in the local economy.

- **Leasing may be another option to extend the buying power** of a district in the short term by expanding the number of instruments and extending the payment for those instruments over a number of years.

- **Stay within your allocated budget.**

2. Each district has specific policies and time frames regarding issuing requisitions and paying invoices. Learn how bills get paid in your district.

- **Generally, a requisition is submitted to your principal, district coordinator or the superintendent.** After receiving administrative approval, a purchase order is issued. A purchase order is a voucher for items specified. The vendor will submit an invoice to you, which you will submit, in turn, to the school secretary or the secretary of the school board. Once the invoice is submitted, approval for payment will be put on the school board agenda as an action item. Some boards handle approvals at each board meeting; some only once a month. Ask your supervisor how your district works. After the school board has authorized payment, the school district will pay the vendor. Knowing the process and handling purchases in a professional and timely manner will assure a good relationship with your vendors.

- **Make sure you have the correct** coding and approvals on requisitions.

- **Follow your district's established procedures** when collecting or expending funds. It is always best to keep your involvement with the handling of money at an absolute minimum. Utilize the appropriate school staff to facilitate the collection of funds as much as possible.

- **Reimbursement** for meals and other professional expenses generally may not exceed a specific dollar amount. For some districts, this is a specific amount per meal; for others it is a per diem. Reimbursements must be pre-approved.

3. Don't try to skirt the rules and regulations.

- **Don't wait until the last minute.**

- **Don't submit partially completed documents** and then expect the business office to complete them.

Student Resale Accounts

Ask your supervisor if it would be possible to establish a resale account for incidentals, including reeds, oils, traps, music books, etc. You will have to provide some of these items if your community doesn't have a local music store.

You can avoid running your resale accounts in the red by staying on top of your record keeping. No matter the amount, *ALWAYS* give receipts for funds collected and provide them to the student immediately. Use receipt books that create copies so that you maintain documentation of all transactions. Deposit funds received as expediently as possible. The teacher is the ultimate responsible official when it comes to handling funds for the music program.

One successful way to run a resale account is to use a **punch card system.** At the beginning of the school year, students purchase a punch card and use the card to purchase the resale items. Try to **avoid handling money directly.** If your school has a school store, inquire if they will handle the resale items. **Purchasing your resale items** from the music representative calling on your school is convenient.

In an Emergency

If you need something right away, the **good working relationship** you have developed with your school music representative can be helpful. He or she will most likely try to assist you.

Sample Purchasing Steps

- **Fill out a requisition** for requested purchases.

- Your principal, business office or superintendent **acts upon this request.**

- **If approved,** a purchase order with a specific number will be issued and sent to the specific store or vendor, or given to you to **initiate the purchase.**

- Merchandise is delivered. The **purchase order number** should appear on the store or vendor invoice.

- **Process the invoice** by first checking that what was received is what was ordered on your original purchase order. Then, immediately forward the invoice to the **school business office** for payment.

- **Payment** to the store or vendor may take 2–4 weeks.

Want more tips for keeping music strong in your schools?
Visit the site devoted to all things music advocacy: **www.supportmusic.com**

The Business Side of Teaching School Music:
Preparing an Instrument Replacement Plan

Consider yourself lucky if you walk into a new job as a director and find adequate equipment in good shape. ***You were chosen to direct the music education program*** in this school. Most superintendents and school boards do not know the importance of ***balanced instrumentation.*** It is up to you to draw up a clear, simple picture of the organization you want to build for your students, and the approximate cost. School boards are composed of people who want ***programs built and organized on a sound foundation.***

4 Steps to Preparing a Proposal for Your Principal, Superintendent and Board of Education for Equipment Purchase or Lease

Step 1. Begin by **evaluating all of your instruments** for condition and value. Using the Inventory Record Template Guide (Exhibit 1), prepare a list of school-owned equipment. List the make of the instrument, condition, approximate age and repairs needed, and estimate its replacement cost and present value. (This value is the trade-in value on new equipment.) You will find your school music dealer representative to be of great assistance in this activity.

Exhibit 1 – Inventory Record Template Guide

Instrument	Inventory Number	Make	Serial Number	New	Date Purchased	Present Value	Present Condition	Remaining Life

Step 2. From the Inventory Record that you have prepared, **prioritize a list of the instruments that should be replaced within the next five years.** Also, add instruments that personnel will require in future years. Keep in mind the probable growth of your department in estimating cost of repairs as well as music supplies and equipment. Use the following guide (*Typical Instrumentation for Bands of Various Sizes*, Exhibit 2) showing suggested instrumentation of various sizes of bands to help choose the proper instruments to purchase.

TIP 8

Exhibit 2 – Typical Instrumentation for Bands of Various Sizes

Instrument	Size of Band				
	35–40	40–50	50–60	60–75	75–90
Flute	4(d)	6(d)	7(d)	10(d)	12(d)
Oboe	1	1	2	2(e)	3(e)
English Horn	1	1			
Bassoon	1	1	2	2	2
B-Flat Clarinet	8	10	12	16	20
Alto Clarinet	0	1	1	1	1
Bass Clarinet	1	1	2	2	2
Contra Bass Clarinet	1	1			
Alto Saxophone	3	5	6	8	9
Tenor Saxophone	1	1	1	2	2
Baritone Saxophone	1	1	1	1	1
Cornet-Trumpet	6	8	8	8	10
French Horn	4	4	4	5	6
Trombone	3	4	4	6	7
Bass Trombone	1	1	1		
Baritone Horn (Euphonium) Sousaphone	2	2	3	3	4
Tuba	2	2	2	2	3
Percussion (including Timpani)	3	4	4	5	6
Total	**40**	**50**	**60**	**75**	**90**

(d) One doubling Piccolo (more for marching bands)
(e) One doubling English Horn

Step 3. Write up a complete five-year plan in a clear, concise manner. The first sheet should be an explanation. Do this in your own words, but be sure to address the reason for the purchase (needs analysis) and how this purchase will help students. Present this rationale to the appropriate supervisor. You may be asked to present the plan to the superintendent or to the school board. If so, have plenty of copies of your proposal available. Refer to the Sample Rationale (Exhibit 3) and make changes to fit your own five-year plan (Exhibits 4 and 5).

Exhibit 3 – Sample Rationale

1. What most likely will be the growth of the band and orchestra in the next five years?

2. What additions must be made to the inventory to satisfy the demand for instruments that will result from this growth?

3. What instruments in the present inventory will need to be replaced?

4. What other materials will be needed in order to provide the students with a quality sequential music education program?

At the end of the five-year period, there will be 60 to 65 instruments in the band inventory, which will allow for increased student participation. To have a balanced instrumentation and offer maximum contribution to school and community activities, this plan would allow for the addition of the following instruments to the inventory:

1 Piccolo	2 Double French Horns
1 Euphonium	1 Oboe
1 Baritone Saxophone	1 Bassoon
2 Mellophones	1 Xylophone
1 Chime	

This plan would also permit the replacement of the following instruments now in the inventory:

1 Double French Horn	1 Tuba
1 Bass Clarinet	1 Tenor Saxophone
1 Euphonium	1 Drum Set
1 Pair Cymbals	1 Marching Snare

The cost for the first three years of the five-year plan is higher because there is an immediate need for several instruments. The last two years show a decline in spending. In making this investment, the school will be able to accommodate the needs of all of the students who choose to be a part of the band program.

Sincerely,

John or Jane Doe

Band Director

Exhibit 4 - Working Paper Template

Schedule A	1st Yr	2nd Yr	3rd Yr	4th Yr	5th Yr
Piccolo					
Oboe					
Other Instruments					
Schedule A Total					

Schedule B					
Misc./Repairs					
Overhauls					
Supplies					
Music					
Schedule B Total					

TIP 8

Exhibit 5 – Estimated Annual Budget for High School Band Program

Schedule A

Instrument	1st Yr	2nd Yr	3rd Yr	4th Yr	5th Yr
C Piccolo	XYZ brand $X,XXX.00				
Oboe		XYZ brand $X,XXX.00			
Bass Clarinet				XYZ brand $X,XXX.00	
Bassoon					XYZ brand $X,XXX.00
Tenor Saxophone	XYZ brand $X,XXX.00				
Baritone Saxophone				XYZ brand $X,XXX.00	
French Horn	XYZ brand $X,XXX.00	XYZ brand $X,XXX.00	XYZ brand $X,XXX.00		
Euphonium	XYZ brand $X,XXX.00		XYZ brand $X,XXX.00		
Tuba			XYZ brand $X,XXX.00		
Xylophone	XYZ brand $X,XXX.00				
Drum Set		XYZ brand $X,XXX.00			
Cymbals			XYZ brand $X,XXX.00		
Marching Snares				XYZ brand $X,XXX.00	
Chimes					XYZ brand $X,XXX.00
Subtotal	$	$	$	$	$

Schedule B

Misc./Repairs					
Overhauls					
Supplies					
Music					
Subtotal	$	$	$	$	$
TOTAL	$	$	$	$	$

TIP 8

Step 4. On the included Depreciation Chart (Exhibit 6), **add all new instruments to be purchased in the future.** Each year, enter the amount of depreciation. Refer to the Expected Life & Depreciation Estimates for Band Instruments (Exhibit 7) to determine the expected life of the instrument. Depreciation for each instrument will be figured using the Average Life column, taking the percentage from the Depreciation Schedule multiplied by the original value of that instrument and subtracting that from the current cost of the instrument.

Exhibit 6 – Depreciation Chart

Instrument	Inv. No.	Value Now	Yr #1	Yr #2	Yr #3	Yr #4	Yr #5	Yr #6	etc.
EX: Instrument #1 (est. life of 10 yrs)	123456	$330	$1,000	$800	$650	$530	$430	$330	

Exhibit 7 – Expected Life & Depreciation Estimates for Band Instruments

Instrument	Should Have an Average Life of	Should Have a Complete Overhaul Every
Flute	15 years	4 years
Oboe & Bassoon	15 years	5 years
Clarinet	10 years	4 years
Alto & Bass Clarinet	15 years	5 years
Saxophone	15 years	5 years
Cornet & Trumpet	10 years	10 years
French Horn	10 years	10 years
Trombone	10 years	10 years
Baritone	15 years	10 years
Tuba & Sousaphone	15 years	10 years
Drums	10 years	10 years

Depreciation Schedule

Year	Estimated Life of 10 Years	Estimated Life of 15 Years
1	20%	20%
2	15%	15%
3	12%	10%
4	10%	8%
5	10%	7%
6	8%	6%
7	8%	6%
8	6%	5%
9	6%	5%
10	5%	4%
11		4%
12		3%
13		3%
14		2%
15		2%

1. Longevity depends greatly upon the quality of the instruments when new. The better-made instruments will stand up and last over a longer period of time.

2. The amount of use and care students give the instruments will have a bearing on the length of usability.

3. Keeping the instrument in good condition through continual minor repairs and periodic overhauls will add to its longevity.

Want more tips for keeping music strong in your schools?
Visit the site devoted to all things music advocacy: **www.supportmusic.com**

TIP 8

Tips for Success is produced by the Music Achievement Council • www.musicachievementcouncil.org • 800.767.6266

The Business Side of Teaching School Music:
Maximizing Fiscal Opportunities

Whether you are a supervisor or a one-person music program, *money is the fuel that keeps the program going.* Try incorporating these strategies and procedures *to maximize your fiscal resources.*

Tips for Community Fund-Raising

- **Make sure the community is well-informed of the need.** A preview article in the local newspaper documenting the need for additional funds for your program is very valuable. If the funds are for a specific purpose (uniforms, travel, instruments, etc.), it is important that the community knows exactly how the money will be spent and that the need is well-substantiated. An article with a picture is great to draw the reader's attention.

- **Make provisions for recognizing donors.** Donors can be recognized with inserts to concert programs or ads in the newspapers. Be creative. Donations can be made "in memory" or "in honor" of someone. Thank you notes sent to donors by students are a must! People are more likely to contribute again if they are thanked the first time.

- **Try to find a unique fund-raising idea.** Lots of groups sell fruit, candy, wrapping paper, etc., but don't be afraid to get more creative. One high school instrumental program held a raffle in which a $1,000 cash prize was awarded at the beginning of each halftime show. It was a great way to start each performance, and the publicity was wonderful.

- **Ask a good cross-section of parents to help.** You cannot organize and hold a fund-raiser on your own. Make sure all segments of the community are included in the process. Everyone needs to feel included.

- **Do not conflict with other fund drives in the community.** Communication is the key. You do not want to cause bad feelings by "stepping on toes." Do not duplicate an idea already used by other organizations. Everyone will gain by working together.

- **Don't forget.** Your booster group should do more than fund-raising. Booster group members can hand out music education information to other community members, give a presentation before a civic group or help in organizing the activities mentioned in the advocacy materials. Information kept to yourself doesn't help anyone—including your students.

Grants

- **Make sure you are getting the full story** as to who can apply for a grant opportunity or for the grant dollars received by your district. A grant to improve reading, or for interdisciplinary instruction, may be able to be used for music. You must know how your content area fits into the bigger academic picture, or how it can support other academic areas. Be especially cognizant of technology funding opportunities.

TIP 9

- **Read the specifications carefully** to see how you can and cannot use funds.

- **Answer the grant questions concisely** and specifically. Follow instructions and meet deadlines.

- **If your district doesn't have a grant writer** and the task falls to you, work with a colleague who has been successful—a grant mentor!

Important Program Practices

- **Maintain a detailed**, accurate and up-to-date inventory of instruments, uniforms and your music library.

- **Have a written instrument and equipment maintenance and replacement program.** This is best accomplished by having a 3–5 year plan, which includes annual amounts for repair budgets, identifying instruments that need to be replaced due to age or condition, and new instruments that need to be added due to growth or changes in the emphasis of your program. The plan should be based on the educational needs and priorities for the music department. Identifying real needs will not only facilitate expenditure of public funds for the program, but will also prepare you to address your program needs when private funds may be available.

- **Consolidate resources and share** within the district or across districts. Partnering with others can make sure you all have the equipment you need. Many grant opportunities require such partnerships or cooperative efforts.

Additional Resources for Music Programs

Parental and Community Support
These are invaluable resources.

- **Don't take this support for granted.** Thank people for their support, including their contributions of time, both publicly and privately. Work to get more people involved to spread out the work equally. Otherwise, the same few will do all the work and burnout will set in. Don't forget to ask parents who no longer have children in the program to continue to support your current students' efforts.

- **Think long-term.** Build relationships and be careful to not burn bridges. You never know what you will need, when and from whom.

Working with Your School Music Dealer

- **The goal of a committed school music dealer is to help music educators** build strong music programs. Collaboration between the school music dealer and music educator can enhance the quality, size and importance of a music program, thereby leading to success.

- **View your school music dealer as a resource.** Some services often provided to music educators and music programs include volume discounts, music folders, quality and timely repair service, emergency loaners, advocacy materials, regular visits and insight into the "ins and outs" of the workings of the school district and community.

More Resources to Access

- **School District Initiatives** (as an example, link into your district's technology program)

- **Booster and Parent Groups**

- **Concert Revenue**

- **Paid Performances**

- **Sale of Tapes and Videos** (Know the copyright law.)

- **Curriculum Consultation for Other Districts**

- **Sale of Equipment** (Check district procedures.)

- **Donations: Parents and Community**

- **Connect to Your Parents' Networks** (Many businesses have foundations that as employees, parents can access.)

- **Service Clubs**

Want more tips for keeping music strong in your schools?
Visit the site devoted to all things music advocacy: **www.supportmusic.com**

 **TIP 9**

Tips for Success is produced by the Music Achievement Council • www.musicachievementcouncil.org • 800.767.6266

Telling the Story:
Great Ways to Get Your Message Out

Regularly scheduled arts events open doors to community education. Concert audiences appreciate informative printed program notes or a presentation offering information about the particular compositions to be performed. Ask your music dealer for assistance with preparation and printing. How about sponsoring a lecture/demonstration on certain pieces or styles of music prior to, or during, a performance? A parent or faculty rhythm band accompanying your school group on an appropriate piece during a concert provides an *engaging experience for all.* Why not ask an audience member to "conduct" a piece that the performers know and can execute quite well?

Ideas to Implement

- **Put facts that support music education** on marquees and community bulletin boards, such as those at banks or grocery stores.
- **Put mailers in monthly credit card statements** from a local department store, or insert with monthly utility bills.
- **Provide recordings of school performance groups** to be played when callers are on hold on the school phone system (obtain all required copyright permissions).
- **Provide music-related statements on "table tents" for restaurants.**
- **Have students write letters inviting community members** to school music programs; program information can accompany the students' invitation.
- **Stage a "music open house"** in which community members are invited to attend regularly scheduled classes.

Broadcast Your Act

Performing Wonders: Kids and the Arts, A Broadcaster Guide to Teaching Children About the Arts offers ideas to help radio or television stations give arts education visibility.

- **Special Report: Arts Education.** For a special news report or series, interview school officials and teachers to learn how schools use the arts as a learning tool.
- **On with the Show.** Follow a student music, dance or drama performance through casting and rehearsals to opening night.
- **Profile Student Artists.** Stations regularly produce "Student Athlete of the Week" features. Why not give the same kind of visibility to student artists?

To Get the Creative Juices Flowing, Consider the Following:

- A performance where a student or history teacher dresses like the composer of the piece and interjects stories of their inspiration or reasons for writing the

TIP 10

piece. Students love to see their teachers participate in these types of activities, plus it involves your faculty directly (thus allowing them to see the benefits of your program firsthand). And it involves student research—an interdisciplinary approach! Your administrators will see you as a real team leader.

- **Another performance for children and parents** could be an informal rehearsal of a quartet staged to demonstrate the collaborative process and exchange of ideas in bringing music to life. Building value for music also means sharing the process, not just the product!

- **Give a presentation on the nature of sound and demonstrate the ways** in which the various instruments create their own unique voice. The activities could include allowing children and parents to "test" each of the instruments. A connection to science!

- **Beginner-of-the-Month Awards.** Music teachers identify one beginning music student each month who has demonstrated significant effort, improvement or collegiality. A traveling trophy goes to the student's school for display. The newspaper runs the student's photo, providing public recognition and increased community awareness. Initially the trophy could be sponsored by the school music dealer.

To assist in recruiting and to help the visual arts and music teachers work together, hold a poster contest each fall and spring. Over a 2–3 week period, students create posters around the theme "Join Band!" or "Join Orchestra!" or "Join Choir!" Teachers select a poster to be displayed in the school. The school music dealer could provide an ice cream party for that student's class. Later, display all the posters at a local bank. Local TV stations love covering this event!

Want more tips for keeping music strong in your schools?
Visit the site devoted to all things music advocacy: **www.supportmusic.com**

Tips for Success is produced by the Music Achievement Council • www.musicachievementcouncil.org • 800.767.6266

Telling the Story:
Communicating with Your Community

To ***better inform the community*** about the purpose, structure and achievements of the school's music program, provide an annual written report to the appropriate supervisor and, with permission, to parents and the community.

Steps to Success in Communicating Goals and Accomplishments

The Content

- **Data! Data! Data!** People are busy, so respect their time by providing easy-to-decipher data about every aspect of your program. Include data on enrollment, program growth, percentage participation within the school, average student GPA, number of performances, number of students participating in Honor Groups, All-State Ensembles, etc. This data should provide measurable information that would be used for comparison in subsequent years. In addition, this will assist you in setting goals for the future.

- **The report could also include** more generalized information about the music program, special community performances and appearances by guest artists. The music program is a wonderful public relations component to the school; administrators know this, so use it to your advantage. Make the school and your students the focus of all of your good news.

- **Use student quotes** about the value of being in your program, and place those quotes strategically in the document. (Be sure to secure written permission to use the quotes.) You could also include quotes from adjudicators, parents and other community notables about how wonderful your program is and its benefits for participating students.

- **Detail every positive contribution** in the school or community—no matter how small— by individuals or groups, students and staff.

The Process

- **Start an annual report file** at the beginning of each school year and add material to it on a daily basis. It is much easier to eliminate excess information than to create it just before the deadline.

- **Sort the entries by useful categories**, such as ensemble types or grade levels. Review each event with the perspective of whether it is a selling point for the program, or an interesting detail for an administrator.

The Format

- **Use a spreadsheet to report your data.** It should be easy to understand at first glance. You may want to show it to a colleague before submitting it to your administration. Remember that the format established for your report will be used in subsequent years to make comparisons and show overall program growth.

- **Consider what appearance the finished report should have.** Think about how many photographs and charts to include and what size the report should be. One standard size is 8-1/2 x 11 inches, which prints on an 11 x 17 sheet that yields four pages. Deal in multiples of four pages. (It is impossible to have an odd number of pages unless one page is blank.) Also consider the **texture and quality of paper** you will use.

- **Secure permission beforehand** if you want to include photographs in your report. Parents must provide written permission for photos of your students to be included.

- It is important that the **report is submitted to your supervisor before** it is distributed elsewhere. Work with this person to determine how best to proceed with additional copies and distribution.

TIP 11

Graphically Appealing

- **Leave enough white space** so that components don't look crammed together.
- **Think about the size of the text** (11 point works well); the space between lines of text (consider a minimum of a 1/2 point larger than the type size)
- **Consider the kind of type style used**—serif versus sans serif—the printer can show you examples of these type styles. Studies have shown reading speed and comprehension are 30 percent better with serif typeface. Avoid using too many different sizes and type styles.
- **Pictures and graphs are appealing.** A small number of photos showing only a few people is better than too many tiny photos or large ones of an entire ensemble. Position photos so the dominant subject looks into the page, not off into space.
- **Pay attention** to page balance.

Organize

- **Before you start writing,** organize
- **Include all pertinent information**
- **Prioritize information**
- **Determine which information can be further illustrated** with charts or graphs, or enhanced by other visuals, such as photos
- **Remember to include information** about the importance of music education to student success

Use the "Write Stuff"

- **Attractive graphics will interest readers,** but the core of any publication is its editorial substance.
- **Write professionally** and have your report proofread before taking it to your administration. Be sure to ask for permission to publish the report beyond the confines of the school and ask for input from your supervisor before you make additional copies for others.
- **Write in simple, direct language** to convey information of significance and interest, but with a meaningful message.
- **Outline first**
- **Use strong action verbs**
- **Use short sentences and paragraphs**
- **Use the active voice**
- **Keep people in mind**
- **Use educational jargon sparingly but appropriately.** It is important that you are seen as up-to-date on all current issues related to education, so use the proper terms. Use quotes when possible. Be concise; avoid wordy descriptions.
- **Select familiar words**
- **Simplify; then simplify again**

- **Check and double-check your grammar and spelling,** then have someone else check it yet again. You will be judged by the quality of this document.
- **Write headlines that say something.** Headlines need to communicate so that the people who scan your report can also learn something. Choose titles and headlines that will give a snapshot of the feeling you want to create.
- **Once you have designed an annual report that seems complete,** ask for comments from a variety of others, including an English teacher, a parent and an administrator, before sending the report to a printer. They may not only find typographical errors, but may suggest something you have overlooked.

Distribution

- **The final step is to distribute the report** to the school board, administrators, parents, feeder schools (and the administrators, music educators and counselors in these buildings), the local media and local politicians. Be sure to inform your supervisor about which people you want to receive your report. Make extras to keep on hand and be sure that the principal's office is provided with extra copies so that they can share them with visitors.
- You can also use the report for background information when applying for grants, or as an internal tool to help assess the program.
- **Consider expanding your distribution to include local service groups,** especially since you may find yourself asking them for financial support in the future. You could also distribute a copy to each visitor to the music department, including student teachers and guest artists. Give copies to real estate agents who might have clients looking for a community with a strong music program.

Project Reminders

- **Have clear goals** for what you want to accomplish by producing an annual report.
- **Enlist the help from other faculty members and students** in producing the report. Communicate your goals and what you are trying to accomplish. Talk with journalism and art faculty to create a team approach to producing the most dynamic, content-driven report possible.
- **Work with a local printing company** in understanding time and cost considerations. Ask for their input, based upon their experience and expertise. Get preliminary cost estimates so that you have an idea of the amount involved for the number of copies you want to distribute.
- Talk with your booster or parents' group to **request funding to accomplish your goals in producing an annual report.**
- **Share the process** with your students so they can learn the importance of telling others about the value of music.

Want more tips for keeping music strong in your schools?
Visit the site devoted to all things music advocacy: **www.supportmusic.com**

TIP 11

Telling the Story:
Advocating for Music

A majority of **those outside the fields of music and the arts** do not understand the whys or the hows concerning the process of arts education. **Provided with a clear understanding** of those whys and hows, and supported by quality arts education in practice, **people begin to realize the value of music and arts education.**

If the school board and district administrators are kept well-informed of the benefits that an education in the arts provide, and if this information is supported by sound classroom practices, chances are that the district will favor decisions that strengthen the programs rather than weakening or eliminating them.

Influencing the Realities in Arts Education

- **Shifting educational priorities and budgeting priorities** means that no music or arts educator can afford to consider his or her program immune to cutbacks. When arts educators fail to prepare for potential problems, or deny the potential threat of being seriously diminished or eliminated, the stage is set for disaster.

- **Being a music educator means much more than teaching music to the students in the music classroom.** It involves educating **EVERYONE** in the school environment—parents, faculty colleagues, administrators and the community at large. It is the educator's job to provide administrators with everything they need to know to effectively advocate for the music program.

Effective Ways to Build the Music Program
Ignorance Isn't Bliss

- **Stay informed**
- **Collect and disseminate information** appropriately
- **Know what is happening** in other parts of the school as well as district-wide
- **Join an arts advocacy organization**

You Gotta Have Friends

- **Know your constituency**
- **Think of students as constituents**
- **Build a communication system**
- **Make sure your constituents know how to reach you**

Simon Says. . .

- **Be prepared**
- **Set up phone and e-mail trees**
- **Keep constituents informed**
- **Disseminate information** on a regular basis
- **Initiate dialogue**
- **Establish** a fine arts booster group
- **Personally invite all constituents** to attend arts events, informances and performances
- **Thank constituents** for attending
- **Invite constituents** into the classroom
- **Provide opportunities to learn** about the process of making music

Get Real!

- **Talk with students about the value** of arts education
- **Discuss with students** what you are teaching
- **Discuss with students** what they are learning
- **Discuss with students** how these skills relate to their real world of school, work and life

Birds of a Feather

- **Be a team player**
- **Be regarded as a leader**
- **Treat your friends** as allies
- **Discuss issues** of mutual concern
- **Remember:** *United we stand, divided we fail*
- **Become a unit**: "The Fine Arts Department"
- **Point out critical interdisciplinary links**
- **Offer to collaborate** with others and to play a key role

Start with a Single Step

- **Get your program** on your school board agenda
- **Know the budget process**
- **Review the school board agenda** several days before every meeting. Look for items that might impact your program (for example: budget cuts, graduation requirements, staffing reductions)

- **Don't assume** that everyone agrees that students need or benefit from an education in the arts
- **Think of advocacy as nothing more** than effective public relations
- **Use advocacy in a positive way**—it's the "good news" about music education
- **Make advocacy a way of life**
- **Advocate daily** with students and teacher colleagues
- **Develop "partnerships"** and collaborations that are win-win
- **Ensure that all constituents realize their responsibility to be good advocates**
- **Equip students to be your best advocates**

Nothing is Carved in Stone

- **Don't assume**—you rarely have all the information.
- **Fatal Assumption #1:** Those you assume are decision-makers, really are decision-makers.
- **Fatal Assumption #2:** The decision-makers will never change their minds.
- **Fatal Assumption #3:** The decision-makers will always stay the same.
- **Fatal Assumption #4:** The environment in which your program exists will always remain the same.
- **Fatal Assumption #5:** The rationale you believe in has universal acceptance.

An Apple a Day

- Know your vulnerabilities
- Work to correct those vulnerabilities

Just a Reminder

The real issues are often about power and the allocation of resources—that spells p-o-l-i-t-i-c-s.

Keep the Focus

Although politics will likely be a component, the focus of arts education advocacy is whether students have access to the quality arts programs they need and deserve.

Want more tips for keeping music strong in your schools?
Visit the site devoted to all things music advocacy: **www.supportmusic.com**

TIP 12

Tips for Success is produced by the Music Achievement Council • www.musicachievementcouncil.org • 800.767.6266

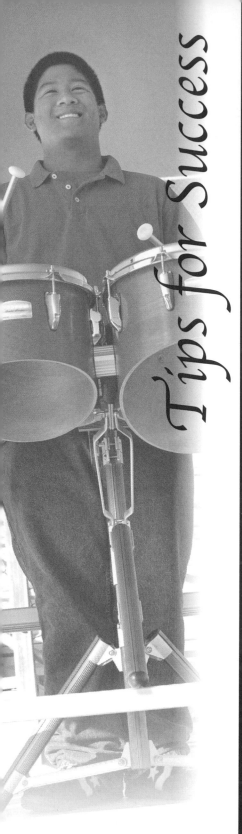

Telling the Story:
Music Impacts Learning and Way of Life

Champions of Change indicates music study improved students' success in math. A new report compiling the results of seven major studies provides important new evidence of enhanced learning and achievement when the arts are an integral part of the educational experience, both in and out of America's K–12 schools.

Champions of Change

Champions of Change: The Impact of the Arts on Learning provides qualitative and quantitative data on the learning and achievement of students involved in a variety of arts experiences. The report was edited by former *New York Times* Education Editor Edward B. Fiske, who is also the author of *Smart Schools, Smart Kids* and the best-selling *Fiske Guide to Colleges.* In an introduction by former U.S. Secretary of Education Richard Riley, the findings are referred to as "groundbreaking," and are offered to "address ways that your nation's education goals may be realized through enhanced arts learning." The *Champions of Change* research offers clear evidence of how the arts can improve academic performance, energize teachers and transform learning environments. Among the findings:

- **Students with a high level of arts participation outperform** "arts-poor" students on virtually every measure. Based on an analysis of the Department of Education's database of 25,000 students, UCLA Graduate School of Education & Information Studies Professor James S. Catterall found that sustained involvement in the arts correlates with success in other subjects and developing positive attitudes about community—both generally and also for children in poverty. The correlation is particularly strong between music and success in math.

- **Intensive involvement in a single discipline** should probably be thought to be even more important developmentally than high levels of more diverse involvement in the arts. A Columbia University study focuses on youngsters who exhibit very high levels of involvement within a single arts discipline over the secondary school years. Researchers report explorations of differences shown by students who were heavily involved in instrumental music. Students concentrating in instrumental music do substantially better in mathematics than those with no involvement in music. Also, low socioeconomic status students with high involvement in music do better than the average student at attaining high levels of mathematics proficiency. Twice as many low socioeconomic status eighth-graders in band and/or orchestra score at high levels in mathematics as did low socioeconomic status eighth-graders with no reported involvement in instrumental music.

- **Arts experiences enhance "critical thinking" abilities and outcomes.** Students preparing for what former Federal Reserve Chairman Alan Greenspan described as America's "economy of ideas," need an education that develops imaginative, flexible and tough-minded thinking. Researchers at the National Center for Gifted and Talented at the University of Connecticut found that students involved

TIP 13

in the arts were motivated to learn not just for test results or other performance outcomes, but also for the learning experience itself.

New Harris Poll Links Music Education to Advanced Studies and Higher Incomes; National Association for Music Education and Artist Steven Van Zandt Endorse Findings; No Child Left Behind Act is Leaving Music Education Behind, Despite Proven Benefits

WASHINGTON, DC (November 12, 2007) – At an event with actor and musician "Little" Steven Van Zandt and MENC: The National Association for Music Education, Harris Interactive today released an independent poll which shows a positive association of music with lifelong educational attainment and higher income. Nearly nine in ten people (88 percent) with post graduate degrees participated in music education. Further, 83 percent of those with incomes higher than $150,000 or more participated in music.

With the No Child Left Behind Act currently up for reauthorization in Congress, a discussion on music education is more important right now than ever. Music is recognized, on paper, as a core academic subject but with actual testing in only a narrow range of subjects, music is usually one of the first programs to be cut.

"Research confirms that music education at an early age greatly increases the likelihood that a child will grow up to seek higher education and ultimately earn a higher salary. The sad irony is that 'No Child Left Behind' is intended to better prepare our children for the real world, yet it's leaving music behind despite its proven benefits," said Dr. John Mahlmann, Executive Director of MENC: The National Association for Music Education. "While music clearly corresponds to higher performing students and adults, student access to music education had dropped about 20 percent in recent years, thanks in large part to the constraints of the No Child Left Behind Act."

Musician, actor and music education activist Steven Van Zandt adds, "Obviously, music is a big part of my life and I've had remarkable experiences as part of the music industry. That is why I am now combining my life's work and my passion for music education. The Harris Poll and other studies like it document the fact that you don't have to be a rock star to benefit from music education. Music benefits everyone in all walks of life. Through my Rock and Roll Forever Foundation, I am working with professional music educators on the development of 'Little Steven's Rock and Roll High School.' This curriculum will be available at no cost to schools and can help future generations learn about music, history, culture and the arts – all through Rock and Roll."

"If you want to be a CEO, college president or even a rock star, the message from this survey is: take music," Mahlmann added. "As with reading, writing and arithmetic, music should be a core academic focus because it is so vital to a well rounded education and will pay dividends later in life, no matter the career path taken."

Respondents of the Harris Poll cite skills they learned in music as helping them in their careers today. Seventy-two percent of adults with music education agree that it equips people to be better team players in their career and nearly six in ten agree that music education has influenced their creative problem solving skills. Many also agree music education provides a disciplined approach to problem solving, a sense of organization and prepares someone to manage the tasks of their job more successfully.

An earlier Harris study shows significantly higher graduation and attendance rates in schools with music programs (90.2 percent compared to 72.9 percent and 93.3 percent compared to 84.9 percent, respectively).

Other studies show the value of music programs to our future generations:

Students in top quality music programs scored 22 percent higher in English and 20 percent higher in math on standardized tests mandated by the No Child Left Behind Act (University of Kansas).

In 2006, SAT takers with coursework in music performance scored 57 points higher on the verbal portion of the test and 43 points higher on the math portion (The College Board, Profile of College-Bound Seniors National Report for 2006).

"Parents, educators, state legislatures and the Congress need to take these studies seriously. This relationship between music education and better performance in life is not accidental. How are we supposed to continue as a creative society without exposing our students to the arts? Rock and Roll shapes our culture and is the great equalizer among people of different racial, social and economic background. It belongs in the schools!" said Van Zandt.

Want more tips for keeping music strong in your schools?
Visit the site devoted to all things music advocacy: **www.supportmusic.com**

TIP 13

Telling the Story:
What Research Shows

Critical Links:

Learning in the Arts and Student Academic and Social Development finds that the arts provide critical links for students to develop crucial *thinking skills and motivations* they need to *achieve at higher levels.* The research studies further suggest that for certain populations—students from economically disadvantaged circumstances, students needing remedial instruction and young children—*the effects of learning in the arts may be especially robust in boosting learning and achievement.*

"I urge education leaders throughout the country to read this compendium and pay close attention to its findings," said G. Thomas Houlihan, Executive Director of the Council of Chief State School Officers (CCSSO), the association of leaders of state departments of education. "In the No Child Left Behind Act, *Congress named the arts as one of the core subjects that all schools should teach.* The studies in *Critical Links* show the wisdom of that decision and the *benefit of arts learning for every child.*" *Critical Links* is available at www.aep-arts.org/publications

Reading and Language Development

- **Basic Reading Skills:** Certain forms of **arts instruction enhance and complement basic reading instruction** by helping children "break the phonetic code" that unlocks written language through the association of letters, words and phrases with sounds, sentences and meanings.

- **Literacy:** Young children who engage in dramatic enactments of stories and text **improve** their **reading comprehension, story understanding and ability to read new materials** they have not seen before. The effects are **even more significant** for children from economically disadvantaged circumstances and those with reading difficulties in the early and middle grades.

- **Writing:** Spatial reasoning skills inherent in learning **music** are **needed for planning and producing writings**. In addition, dramatic enactments by young children are shown to produce more effective writing. Learning experiences in dance also lead to the development of expressive and reflective skills that enhance writing proficiency.

Mathematics

Certain music instruction, including comprehensive instruction that includes training in keyboard skills, has been shown to develop spatial reasoning and spatial-temporal reasoning skills, which are **fundamental to understanding and using mathematical ideas and concepts.**

TIP 14

Fundamental Cognitive Skills and Capacities

Learning in **individual art forms** as well as in **multi-arts experiences engages and strengthens such fundamental cognitive capacities** as spatial reasoning (the capacity for organizing and sequencing ideas); conditional reasoning (theorizing about outcomes and consequences); problem solving; and the components of creative thinking (originality, elaboration, flexibility).

Motivation to Learn

Motivation and the **attitudes** and **dispositions to pursue and sustain learning** are essential to achievement. **Learning in the arts nurtures** these capacities—active engagement, disciplined and sustained attention, persistence and risk-taking—and increases attendance and education aspirations.

Effective Social Behavior

Studies of **student learning experiences** in drama, music, dance and multi-arts activities **show student growth** in self-confidence, self-control, self-identity, conflict resolution, collaboration, empathy and social tolerance.

School Environment

It is critical that a school provide a positive context for learning. Studies in the compendium show that the **arts** help to **create** the kind of **learning environment** that is **conducive to teacher and student success** by fostering teacher innovation, a positive professional culture, community engagement, increased student attendance and retention, effective instructional practice and school identity.

Want more tips for keeping music strong in your schools?
Visit the site devoted to all things music advocacy: **www.supportmusic.com**

TIP 14

Tips for Success is produced by the Music Achievement Council • www.musicachievementcouncil.org • 800.767.6266

Telling the Story:
Proactive is Better than Reactive

With the reduction of funding for educational programs on many levels, and with the unprecedented pressures put on schools, districts and states by the No Child Left Behind Act, *responsibility for retaining arts programs* rests with every arts educator, every parent and all community members.

It's Always about Politics

Today's education and political environments require the **need to demonstrate political skills when advocating for the importance of arts programs.** We need to **train ourselves and others in school politics** to **ensure student-centered decisions.** Parents and community members must be reminded that the school district belongs to them. It's much easier to **influence a decision that hasn't yet been made** (proactive) than to undo a decision (reactive) that the players within the system see as final. **The key to being proactive is to be informed and organized!**

Know the Process

- It is critical that you understand the **timeline and process by which decisions** are made in your school district. Your goal is to influence key decisions before they are made.

- Determine the normal practice in your district—who or what body is the **primary decision-maker, when do they make their decisions** and **where do they get their information?**

- Know what your **state law requires** regarding instruction and accreditation.

- Recognize the **distinction between decision-makers and decision drivers**. The decision-makers will nearly always take their cues from the decision drivers. Know what and/or who are the decision drivers in your district.

- **Waiting** until "something" happens can be **deadly.**

Power in Numbers

- Without the involvement of the community, **decisions tend to be driven by adult issues**—salary, teaching schedules, education reforms or money.

- Every individual in the community has a right to be involved in the process. This is the **major reason for organizing** a Fine Arts Support Group—to **broaden your political power.** Numbers speaking in a **unified voice** are much louder than a small group of angry parents.

- If the board and administration understand that the **majority of their constituents support** a strong arts program, they will be **less likely to make decisions that weaken those programs.**

TIP 15

Be Organized

- Start with arts educators. **Maintain unity.** A lack of unity makes teachers susceptible to the "divide-and-conquer" game.

- Recognize that the decision-making process is usually adult-centered and thus political. **Political situations require political solutions.**

- Expand your **parent support group.** Include parents of younger children who may not yet have had the opportunity to participate in arts programs.

- **Know the parents and community:** Who are the organizers, the persuaders and the speakers?

- Develop and maintain **communication mechanisms:** mailing lists; rapid-call telephone tree and e-mail tree; Web site; arts newsletter.

- **Maintain annual long-term statistical data** to provide a profile of student involvement and the financial viability of the program. (Refer to *Tips for Success,* #3.)

- **Celebrate accomplishments** of the program and **document** them for presentation to administration, parents and community in the form of **concert inserts** and an **annual report.** (Refer to *Tips for Success,* #11.)

- **Establish positive relationships** with members of the school board.

- Make sure there is **representation at all school board meetings;** review the agenda several days prior to the meeting.

- **Stay informed of all administrative proposals.** Communicate the content and possible impact to support groups.

- The parent group may choose to **recruit, support and elect school board members and legislators** who support arts education.

- Review *Tips for Success,* #12.

Remember:

- Arts educators **cannot afford to be isolationists.**

- Arts educators **must take time** to establish administrative, parental and community connections and relationships.

- Arts educators **must make unified decisions** that ensure an arts education for all students.

- Arts educators must **keep the focus on: "What is best for the students?"**

In a Time of Crisis...

- **Identify the issues:** Which are adult-centered? Which are student-centered? What is really driving the decision?

- **Separate the issues** and consider which ones are most important to the overall solution.

- **Define the issues** from the perspective of short- and long-term effects on students, curriculum and budget.

- **Examine each issue** carefully, looking for secondary issues. Are you dealing with educational reform, a financial crisis, legislative mandate or some other issue?

- **Where is the decision made?** Superintendent? Principal? School board?

- **Develop impact statements:** These are responses that demonstrate in tangible ways what the long-term effect of a proposal will be on student learning, the curriculum, student opportunities to participate and the district budget.

- **Never volunteer cuts to other programs!**

Want more tips for keeping music strong in your schools?
Visit the site devoted to all things music advocacy: **www.supportmusic.com**

TIP 15

Tips for Success is produced by the Music Achievement Council • www.musicachievementcouncil.org • 800.767.6266

Tips for Success

Telling the Story:
What Administrators Can Do

Your administrative team—principal and superintendent—allocate time and resources for instruction. Their support is critical to developing a climate in which your arts program can grow. Administrators need your help in making the music program successful. It is the job of the music educator to provide administrators with everything they need to know to be an advocate for the program. Arts educators must therefore equip administrators with this type of information. This will allow your supervisors to speak knowledgeably about the inherent value of students participating in your arts program.

Don't assume that administrators have all the information that you possess at your fingertips. They do not. **It is the responsibility of the arts educators** to pass along the information received so that administrators remain up-to-date with research results and current studies.

When you succeed, your principal succeeds! Share the following ideas with your administrative team to ensure that your music education program flourishes.

Quality Instruction

- **Provide** music education opportunities for all students.
- **Ask:** Is your district's program about providing comprehensive music education or providing entertainment for school and community events?
- **Provide** all music classes with certified music educators. Recruit and hire competent teachers, asking current music teachers for assistance in the interview process.
- **Support** music education as an integral part of the curriculum, providing music educators with the opportunity to work together to plan a sequential pre-K through grade 12 music curriculum. Based on the National Standards for Music Education, the curriculum will describe what students should know and be able to do at the end of grades 4, 8 and 12, as well as stating how and when that knowledge will be assessed and evaluated. It should also include teaching strategies to help students attain specified performance levels.
- **Coordinate** class schedules to minimize conflicts of music classes with other courses.
- **Ensure** that student grades for music courses are weighted in the GPA—the same way as grades for other academic courses.
- **Provide** a music program budget that includes funding for staffing, instruments, maintenance and repair, purchase of music and current technology.
- **Encourage** staff to be professionally active by providing support to serve in leadership positions, to attend professional meetings and to actively participate in professional development opportunities.
- **Provide** conflict-free time for music events in the school calendar. The needs of teachers, coaches, parents and students must be given equal consideration.

- **Show** your support by attending concerts. Drop by the rehearsal the next day to talk with the students.

- **Visit** music classrooms. This is where the learning celebrated at the concert takes place. Observe the process and provide feedback to your music teachers often.

- **Share** with your staff members the research regarding effective techniques for improving student learning.

- **Value your Music Education Department.** They can bring notoriety to your school and build spirit among students and staff.

- **Read** current literature. This should include the role of the arts in student achievement (for example: Eric Jensen's *Art with the Brain in Mind,* ASCD, 2001).

- **Encourage** staff to organize and plan effectively. This includes lesson plans, communication with parents and community, classroom structure and discipline management.

- **Be available** to discuss opportunities and issues as they develop.

- **Encourage** your music teachers to connect with teachers in other disciplines.

Community Awareness

- *Gaining the Arts Advantage* (available at www.aep-arts.org/Publications) states that the **No. 1 factor** in creating support for arts education is **community involvement.**

- **Communicate** to others the many music education opportunities that are available in your school. Know how these opportunities compare to those in other surrounding districts of similar size.

- **Track** music enrollment statistics by the number of participants and percentage participating. Annually review those numbers with your staff to monitor student satisfaction and enrollment trends.

- **Invite** parents and community members to visit music classrooms and observe the process of music education; always be looking for ways for your music educators to extend their programs beyond the classroom.

- **Know** the instructional needs of your programs in terms of time, resources and the number of students served. Share this information with the school board, parents and the community frequently.

- **Make** presentations or invite arts advocates to speak at PTA and community meetings (such as those of service organizations) to share the importance of music education for students.

- **Know and communicate** the benefits of sequential curricular music education.

Further Your Understanding

- **Become familiar** with the ways participation in music education develops creativity, promotes higher-order thinking skills, enhances sensitivity and understanding of self, instills disciplined work habits and correlates with gains in standardized test scores.

- **Stay abreast** of current trends in music education by regularly reviewing Web sites such as:
  www.supportmusic.com
  www.aep-arts.org
  www.artsedge.kennedy-center.org
  www.awesomelibrary.org
  www.amc-music.org
  www.carts.org
  www.childrensmusicworkshop.com/advocacy
  www.cmea.ca
  www.educationindex.com/music
  www.menc.org
  www.mtlc.net
  www.musicachievementcouncil.org
  www.musiceducationconsultants.net
  www.music-for-all.org
  www.mustcreate.org
  www.nyphilkids.org
  www.schoolmusicmatters.com
  www.smartz.org
  www.uk.cambridge.org
  www.usamusic.org
  www.weallneedmusic.ca

Share Your Vision!

- **Collaborate** with your administrative colleagues and faculty to support standards-based arts education.

- **Articulate** the role and value of arts education to the total educational experience. Insist that arts educators support the school's total educational vision.

- **Provide** time for educators to develop and deliver integrated learning opportunities.

- **Encourage** fellow administrators, teachers in other disciplines and parents to read about and understand the process of arts education. Include information in your school newsletter, on fact sheets that can be handed out at open house evenings and at parent-teacher conferences, as well as in school activity programs and mailings.

- **Invite** arts educators to make presentations regarding the value and process of music education at administrative conferences and as part of teacher in-service days.

- **Include** articles in individual school and school district newsletters that communicate the value of arts education in a student's education and preparation for the future.

Want more tips for keeping music strong in your schools?
Visit the site devoted to all things music advocacy: **www.supportmusic.com**

 **TIP 16**

Tips for Success is produced by the Music Achievement Council • www.musicachievementcouncil.org • 800.767.6266

Supporting Music Education:
Critical Factors for a Successful Program

If you are looking to maintain, build or expand your music program, *Gaining the Arts Advantage: Lessons from Schools that Value Arts Education* examines 13 critical factors that influence successful arts programs. Consider the following factors as a self-assessment and analyze the extent to which the following critical factors are present in your school district.

Factor 1: The Community

The No. 1 factor for creating support for arts education is community networking and involvement. In districts with strong arts education programs, the community—broadly defined as parents and families, artists, arts organizations, businesses, local civic and cultural leaders, and institutions—is actively engaged.

School administrators in these districts encourage and support:

- **active parent and community involvement** in school arts programs
- **interdisciplinary teams** involving arts educators in the development of curricula
- **arts faculty involvement** in community arts events
- **artist residencies**
- **student exhibitions and performances** for community audiences

Factor 2: The School Board

- School districts with strong arts education programs have boards of education that provide a supportive policy framework and environment for the arts. Typically, the boards:
- **adopt written policies that value the arts** as equal to other school subjects
- **support** the development of plans to strengthen arts education, then **allocate resources** in accordance with the plan
- **treat arts education equally** with other subject areas if budget cuts are required
- **consider the artistic qualities** of buildings and the needs of arts education programs during facility renovation and development

Factor 3: The Superintendent

Superintendents who regularly articulate a vision for arts education are critically important to the successful implementation and stability of the overall program.

Superintendents interviewed:

- regularly **articulate**—in writing, memos and speeches—the importance of the arts in achieving the goals of the school district
- **appoint** highly effective district-wide arts coordinators

- **develop** a shared understanding with district arts coordinator(s) about the role of arts education
- **provide support** for development and implementation of standards-based arts curricula
- **encourage education staff to collaborate** among disciplines to ensure district-wide initiatives apply to and include the arts
- **commit personal time** to meeting with the arts education personnel of their district and to representatives from the arts and cultural organizations of the community
- **attend arts events**

Factor 4: Continuity

- There is enough continuity in the school and community leadership to implement a comprehensive, long-term arts-education plan
- **Stability in formal leadership** is important in pursuing a set of education goals
- **Strong community traditions** that embrace the arts are important factors in shaping a consensus supporting arts education. School leaders told the researchers that this consensus was a key to program continuity.

Factor 5: The District Arts Coordinator

District arts coordinators facilitate program implementation throughout a school system and maintain an environment of support for arts education. Smaller districts often lack resources for a full-time coordinator, and add the responsibility to the workload of a district curriculum specialist or an arts educator at a school.

Effective coordinators play a number of crucial roles and provide several vital services:

- Arts coordinators are often the staff member most actively **engaged** with influential segments of the community that value the arts and are instrumental in **nurturing and mobilizing community support** for arts education.
- Board members credit arts coordinators with keeping **"the arts on the table"** during budget sessions.
- Coordinators negotiate between board and central office policies and school-level decision-making, an increasingly critical role as districts move toward site-based management.
- Arts coordinators often participate with school-level leadership in the **screening and hiring** of teachers.

- Teachers cite the role of district coordinator in **facilitating communication** among individual schools and in **fostering the climate of support** for arts education in the community and district.

Factor 6: A Cadre of Principals

School principals who collectively support the policy of arts education for all students often are instrumental in the policy's successful district-wide implementation.

- Principals create **the expectations and climate** in the school building, and their support for arts education is essential. For a district as a whole to sustain the successful implementation of arts education for all of its students, a sufficient number of these **building-level leaders must personally value the arts or be persuaded by other pragmatic considerations** to make them an important aspect of the school.
- Many principals spoke of **early learning** or **involvement in the arts** or of **professional development opportunities** that helped them to decide to support arts in their schools.
- Other principals were convinced by the **effectiveness of arts education** in addressing specific issues.
- Principals looking to create **a thematically focused or interdisciplinary approach** in an elementary or middle school have found that art forms can play a central role because of their **complex content and range of activities.**
- Some principals have found that **hard-to-reach students** become **actively engaged** in the arts and, subsequently, in other aspects of the school.

Factor 7: The Teacher as Artist

Effective teachers of the arts are allowed to—indeed, are encouraged to—continue to learn and grow in mastery of their art form as well as in their teaching competence.

- The presence of arts educators in a school has proven time and again to make the difference between **successful, comprehensive, sequential arts education** and those programs in development. What the study found compelling is the **vibrancy** that teachers who practice their art bring to a program that's already strong.
- In the strongest district, this commitment to the teacher as artist is reflected in **recruitment** and **hiring practices** that include auditions and portfolio reviews to assess the applicant's competence in the art form. Experienced arts teachers in the district participate in these reviews.

TIP 17

Tips for Success is produced by the Music Achievement Council • www.musicachievementcouncil.org • 800.767.6266

Factor 8: Parent/Public Relations

School leaders in districts with strong, system-wide arts education programs seize opportunities to make their successes known throughout the community in order to maintain support and secure additional funding.

- Principals told researchers that **parents** who never come to school for parent-teacher conferences **will come to see their child perform, creating opportunities for building relationships** important to the school and district.

Factor 9: An Elementary Foundation

Strong arts programs in elementary school years are the foundation for strong system-wide programs.

- **Elementary programs establish a foundation** in the arts **for all students**, not just for those in specialized programs or those who choose an arts course of study in high school.

- The arts have proven to be **strong components** in the adoption of an **interdisciplinary curriculum** by elementary schools.

- School leaders find, too, that beginning programs in the early years **builds relationships** with parents and community organizations important to **sustaining their support** for comprehensive arts education.

Factor 10: Opportunities for Higher Levels of Achievement

School leaders in these districts provide specialized arts programs as part of their broad strategy for securing and sustaining community support for the district's overall educational goals.

- These programs create an **environment of excellence** that challenges teachers to continue to develop proficiency in their art forms and encourages students to aspire to professional levels of performance.

- **Students** studying arts in these specialized programs expressed to interviewers their **intense pride in, and commitment to, their work.** Their achievements **contribute to community enthusiasm** for the arts and a **belief in the excellence and quality** of the district's educational system.

Factor 11: National, State and Outside Forces

Many districts in this study employ state or national policies and programs to advance arts education.

- **Policies, mandates and funding** from the state or national levels **will not, of themselves**, forge the community/ school consensus required for district-wide arts education. Leaders in districts examined marshaled such forces to strengthen the consensus to support policies and programs in the schools.

- National and state standards for arts education, state education reform movements, federal funding for general school improvement or targeted programs or populations were all used to support and advance arts education in these districts.

Factor 12: Planning

School leaders in this study advise the adoption of a comprehensive vision and plan for arts education, but recommend its implementation incrementally.

- Leaders at the district and building levels repeatedly told researchers that it was important to combine a **compelling vision** of the importance of arts education with a **thoughtful implementation plan** that showed how resources would be apportioned over time to reach all schools and students.

- The **plan established confidence** among arts teachers and building-level administrators that resources would be made available.

Factor 13: Continuous Improvement

School districts that succeed in advancing arts education promote reflective practices at all levels of the schools to improve quality.

- While researchers found few districts using student assessments in the arts as part of a formal accountability system, the **strongest districts** actively encourage the **use of arts assessment** techniques for **improving student, teacher and administrative performance.**

- What researchers observed in these districts was the disposition to **reflect on and improve practice, which** is central to **improving student achievement.**

To read more:

www.supportmusic.com
www.menc.org

TIP 17

Critical Factors: The Importance of "Informed Leadership"

- **The Community** is actively engaged within the schools.

- **The School Board** provides a supportive policy framework and environment for the arts.

- **The Superintendent** regularly articulates a vision for arts education.

- **A Cadre of Principals** – primary instructional leaders at the school level – are instrumental in supporting the policy of arts education for all students.

- **The District Arts Coordinator** facilitates program implementation and maintains an environment of support for arts education.

- **Parent/Public Relations** – seize opportunities to make your program known throughout the community in order to secure support and funding.

- **Continuity in Leadership** means there is enough continuity in the school and community leadership to implement comprehensive arts education.

Critical Factors: The Importance of "Education Content"

- **Planning:** the adoption of a comprehensive arts education vision and its incremental implementation plan.

- **An Elementary Foundation:** strong arts programs in the elementary schools are the foundation for strong system-wide programs.

- **Opportunities for High Levels of Achievement:** provide an environment of excellence and opportunity.

- **The Teacher as Artist:** teachers are encouraged to continue to learn and grow in mastery of their art as well as in their teaching competence.

- **National, State and Other Outside Forces:** state or national policies and programs are employed to advance arts education.

- **Continuous Improvement:** reflective practices at all levels of the schools promote improved quality.

Want more tips on keeping music strong in your schools?
Visit the site devoted to all things music advocacy: **www.supportmusic.com**

TIP 17

Tips for Success is produced by the Music Achievement Council • www.musicachievementcouncil.org • 800.767.6266

Supporting Music Education:
The Art of Teaching

The following examples, offered by one of America's foremost music educators, provide guidance and affirmation of the roles and responsibilities we as music educators all must possess, model and promote. ***Reflections on the Cutting Edge of Teaching: Where Teacher Meets the Pupil*** captures the heart of teaching.

Miss DeLay, as she is invariably known (though long married), has been teaching at the Julliard School for more than half a century, and her former pupils include Itzhak Perlman, Sarah Chang, Midori and Kennedy, Gil Shaham, Robert McDuffie, ChoLiang Lin and Shlomo Mintz. Success like this will, of course, breed success. Students will use their best endeavors to take lessons from the star teacher. Parents will push their gifted offspring her way. Managers will look to her to be training the next prodigy.

But there must be a lot more to it than that. Exceptional young musicians are often delicate seeds; they need teachers with special talents to make them grow. What those talents are, in Miss DeLay's case, have until now been a mystery. Now 83, she has never sought publicity, nor has she published memoirs or a description of her methods. For more than a decade, though, she was closely observed by Barbara Lourie Sand, whose resulting book, *Teaching Genius: Dorothy DeLay and the Making of a Musician* (Amadeus Press), at last opens the door to Miss DeLay's studio. Miss DeLay, it turns out, has no secrets. What she does have is a sound grasp of some basic rules that can be applied to any kind of training.

- **Teach the student, not the subject.** The approach has to be tuned not just to the students' accomplishments but also to their personalities. In some cases, Miss DeLay—mystifying most of her pupils—has seen a trait worth developing in someone even though that person is not going to become a professional musician. The person is paramount.

- **Expect a lot.** What you teach—information and principles but also, and more important, habits and disciplines of thought and practice—will have to last a lifetime. Miss DeLay explains how, at the start of her teaching career, she imagined a circle of exacting listeners sitting in on her classes: Toscanini, Heifetz and others. What would they want to hear? How would they respond? From this exercise came the rigorous program she gives her pupils to take them through their five hours of daily practice.

- **Be positive.** Fear is a strong incentive, but only for as long as the teacher is part of the pupil's life. Encouragement lasts forever. (Isaac Stern suggests that Miss DeLay's characteristic endearments—"Sugarplum," "Sweetie"—covered the problem of not being able to remember so many names when she was seeing dozens of students each week. But the cuddliness—partly a front, of course—helps pupils feel that their teacher is on their side.)

TIP 18

- **Ask questions.** This is where negativity comes in, but subtly. By questioning students, the teacher invites them to think about what they are doing and why. In time, they may start to discover their own faults and find other ways of doing things. They may come to teach themselves.

- **Learn.** Making the lesson a dialogue has another advantage—that the student may start to teach the teacher—at least in how to teach. Teaching is about giving but also gaining.

- **Be yourself; or if not that, at least be someone.** Having a distinctive teacher makes the lesson special. A lot of Miss DeLay's success may be owed to the scarf she always wears around her shoulders.

- **Break down problems.** Students learn little from being told—in however positive a way—that they have done something wrong. And they learn nothing from being told or shown the "right" way. The teacher has to analyze, has to detect just what is going amiss and why.

- **Let progress show.** Miss DeLay, like all other music teachers, marks her students' copies of their pieces to indicate details that need attention. She then thoroughly erases those markings as the problems get solved. Perfection is the clean copy.

- **Do not shun trickery.** Ms. Sand reports the nice story of a boy who said he could not possibly manage the speed Miss DeLay asked for at a certain point in a piece. So she put the metronome away and just asked him to play the passage over and over, a little bit faster each time; lo and behold, he was attaining the impossible.

- **Remember what cannot be taught—but not so as to relax your efforts.** However much they are given good examples, encouraged and taught to question, some students will go farther than others. Innate talent is an issue here but so is innate determination. There are parts of students' minds that cannot be reached, though they may be released.

- **Be a team player.** Miss DeLay works with colleagues who take care of part of the instruction process, and she recognizes the importance of parents, especially where young children are concerned. Nothing will be achieved unless at least one parent is backing the teacher and promoting good attitudes toward work at home.

- **Attend to everything.** Nothing is beneath the teacher. Nothing is beyond the teacher's competence to care. Miss DeLay's pupils have the benefit of her advice in everything from concert dress to relationships with managers.

- **It never ends.** Not only does Miss DeLay make a point of hearing her ex-pupils perform whenever she can, but they clearly know, to judge from the evidence assembled in Ms. Sand's book, that they have been marked by her for life.

Paul Griffith's interview appeared in *The New York Times* on September 3, 2000. Reprinted with permission.

Editor's Note: Dorothy DeLay was one of the world's great teachers and mentor to several generations of violinists. Having had the personal privilege to meet Miss DeLay and observe her teaching, I can only say I was humbled. Miss DeLay passed away in March 2002.

Want more tips for keeping music strong in your schools?
Visit the site devoted to all things music advocacy: **www.supportmusic.com**

TIP 18

Tips for Success is produced by the Music Achievement Council • www.musicachievementcouncil.org • 800.767.6266

Supporting Music Education:
Work with the Best!

Teaching is a people business. Identifying and hiring the best-prepared and motivated candidates for a position is the most important thing we can do for our students, our programs and ourselves. *A thorough hiring process,* one that reflects the care and concern you and your administration have for your program, *is to everyone's benefit.*

What You Can Do—Get Involved!

- **Express an interest in participating** in the hiring process.

- **Be familiar** with your district's policies and practices. They will guide all steps in the hiring process. You may or may not be able to be involved directly in hiring. At the very least, you can be an advocate for your district's music programs by spreading the word about vacancies and encouraging quality candidates to apply.

- A key component of successful programs is that they are based on a team concept where student talents are developed sequentially through K–12 articulation. This only happens in an environment of effective, ongoing communication among staff and administration.

Recruiting

- The ideal situation is one where the district is looking for outstanding candidates on a regular basis. Recruitment is an area where you can have great influence. Spread the word. **Personal contacts are critical!**

- Request that the district **advertise openings in local and regional papers as well as in professional journals.**

- **Post the vacancy** on state **e-mail bulletin boards**. A number of **Internet sites** also post vacancies.

- Send letters to **college placement offices** to ensure applications from recent graduates and experienced alumni.

- **Network with colleagues** and through your **professional organizations.**

- **Contact college music education departments and officers of your state music organizations.**

- Take advantage of bulletin boards or forms to **post vacancies at state and national conventions.**

Screening the Applications

Your recruiting has generated a stack of résumés and applications. Now what? **The résumé** is a succinct record of skills and accomplishments. You **are searching for** past experiences that are good indicators of future success.

- **Recent college graduate résumés** will have a different look than those from experienced professionals. **Key indicators** include leadership positions held,

TIP 19

activities in service organizations (musical/non-musical) and involvement in department/campus organizations. Grades, music awards and individual achievements are important, but the best prospective teachers often have a background rich in people-oriented activities. **The experienced teacher's résumé** will include additional schooling and a listing of recent responsibilities, accomplishments and recognitions.

- **Different is not necessarily bad.** You may find you are drawn to candidates who can do more than one thing. They are often the most talented and offer you the greatest flexibility for the future.

- **The ideal screening session** would have two or more people sorting the applications into individual "Yes," "No" and "Maybe" piles. They would then compare results and discuss differences until reaching a consensus.

- It is again important to bring the **element of personal contact** into the process. At best, screening is an imprecise art prone to unfortunate oversights. A phone call to **a colleague can help you** see a résumé in an entirely different light. This is also the time when a phone call to a reference or colleague can save you considerable time and effort. **Thoroughly checking references before** extending the invitation to interview can give you a good feeling for whether or not the person is right for the position.

Interviewing

- Often, candidates for teaching positions in music are interviewed and selected by principals or other administrators who possess a limited background in music. If that is your situation, **share** *Choose to Teach Music* **with your principal**. These materials can help your principal ask better questions and hopefully make a more informed decision. It might also **get him or her thinking** about including you in the process!

- **A comprehensive interview** should always include **performance assessment** in addition to the standard interview questions. The performance assessment should include performing on major instruments, demonstrating piano keyboard skills, conducting and singing. Performance in specialty areas such as guitar for classroom music, or woodwind, brass, percussion or strings for instrumental positions could be included. Often, **a truer picture of a candidate's strengths and weaknesses** is learned in a few minutes of performance than from an hour of questions and answers.

- **Portfolios** have long been a staple in the visual arts and are becoming a more common requirement among all disciplines. Many recent graduates will have developed portfolios as part of their senior year requirements. These **offer excellent insight** into a student's or experienced professional's skills, achievements, creativity and work habits.

The Final Test

- The top candidate is usually selected after a series of interviews and offered the position. **Stop! Can this candidate be successful working with your students in your district?** The best way to find the answer is by asking him or her to conduct a rehearsal or teach a class. **While there are never any guarantees,** this is the most **critical part of the process** to ensure that you have found the right person. **Do whatever it takes** to make this happen. Recruit a group of students to serve as a summer interview ensemble, promise pizza or offer one of your classes for the demonstration lesson.

- In most cases, a candidate's performance will only affirm your beliefs. However, a significant number of candidates are great in the interview and stumble when actually in the classroom. **Time invested now may save you and your administrator days of frustration in the future.** Ideally, all candidates would be given this opportunity. Then, you would also be in a better position to find that teacher who has weak interview skills but is superb when working with students.

Supporting Music Education:
Helping Teachers Succeed

Mentoring is a ***powerful approach to help new teachers*** be successful in their first years of teaching. The strength of the program lies in the support and assistance of the trained mentors—colleagues of the new teachers who have a wealth of experience, skills and resources to provide support.

What is a Mentoring Program?

- A mentoring program provides new teachers with a structured format for **planning and improving instruction.** It is different from an orientation, which covers the rules and regulations of the teaching assignment.

- Many state departments of education require the services of a mentor as **part of licensing** requirements for beginning teachers.

- A well-organized and smoothly functioning mentoring program requires **careful planning.** Individuals should know their roles and be prepared or trained to assume them. They should have adequate materials and time to engage successfully in the mentoring process.

Everyone Wins

- Participating in mentor training and serving as a mentor are **professionally rewarding activities** for the mentor.

- The long-term results of the mentor/new teacher relationship can **benefit students of both teachers.**

Selection Criteria for Mentors

Being a subject-area expert doesn't necessarily make a person a good teacher; being a good teacher doesn't necessarily make a person a good mentor. The **relationship established between the mentor and the new teacher is the most important** element for a successful mentoring program.

Mentors must be:

- Willing to devote the time and energy to participate in a community of learners with the **goal of improving student learning.**

- **Aware of adult learning needs and the developmental processes of new teachers.**

- Able to **guide colleagues** in identifying problems and possible solutions through cognitive coaching rather than by telling them how to change.

- **Open to new ideas and new ways** to solve problems.

- Able to **see both long- and short-range goals.**

- **Trustworthy, empathetic, open-minded and free from prejudice.**

TIP 20

The Mentor Selection Process

- A pool of mentors should be trained before assignments are made. Since the mentor training provides **valuable professional development for the mentors,** they will learn from the experience even if they don't serve as mentors immediately.

- **Inform the mentor** as to whether mentor compensation is tangible (stipend) or intangible (professional prestige).

- Ideally, the mentors and new teachers should be **matched by subject or grade level and located within the same school.**

- The **best mentor for a new art, music or theater teacher might well be another art, music or theater teacher, even if that person is not in the same school.** Communication between physically distant matches can be facilitated by easy access to phone or e-mail.

Familiarizing New Teachers with the Mentor Program

New teachers **need to be fully informed** about the program in advance, in order to **reduce any feelings of fear or discomfort** about having a more experienced colleague providing feedback to them.

Scheduling Time for Mentoring

- As a guideline, a **minimum of one hour per week** needs to be set aside to allow the mentor and the new teacher to work together.

- The **details of how** mentors and new teachers find time to work together **will vary.**

- **Administrators play a key role** in facilitating the arrangement of time for the mentoring program.

Mentoring and Teacher Evaluation: The Distinctions

- The mentoring program provides a **reflection of teaching—** feedback from a trusted colleague for the **purpose of supporting ongoing professional development.**

- These reflections are **built on high levels of trust** between the new teacher and the mentor, and the mentee must have confidence that the **mentor will not betray that trust** to the administrator.

- The relationship with a mentor must be free from the fear of negative consequences for honesty.

- The mentoring program **should not be confused with evaluation** of a supervisor for the purpose of continuing employment.

Role of the Administrator

- The administrator **manages the details** of implementation and fosters an attitude of support for the mentoring program within the school.

- Administrators must be willing to **dedicate the time, resources and energy necessary** for the program to be successful.

- Administrators should **introduce the mentoring program to the entire school staff.** Staff members who are not directly involved in the program will be **more apt to support the program and its participants if they know** who is doing what, when and why.

Tell People What You Are Doing!

- Showcase the program as an example of the district's **commitment** to supporting new teachers in order **to develop and retain the best.**

- **When hiring new teachers, mention the mentoring program** as an example of the district's commitment to supporting new teachers.

- **Make arrangements for candidates** to meet with a new teacher and mentor to learn about the program firsthand.

- The **mentoring program** may provide the **competitive edge in recruiting** a highly qualified candidate.

Want more tips for keeping music strong in your schools?
Visit the site devoted to all things music advocacy: **www.supportmusic.com** **TIP 20**

Tips for Success is produced by the Music Achievement Council • www.musicachievementcouncil.org • 800.767.6266

Supporting Music Education:
Expanding the Learning Power of Music

The contemporary student comes to the classroom with a sophisticated knowledge of computers. It is vital that we creatively approach and utilize the application of available technology to *engage students and enhance learning.* Multimedia learning provides teachers, including music teachers, the *opportunity to be at the core of communications.*

What is Multimedia Learning?

● Not long ago, **Steve Jobs, one of the inventors of personal computing and co-founder and CEO of Apple,** said, "The medium of our times is video (sound) and photography, but most of us are still consumers as opposed to being 'authors.' **The drive over the next 20 years is to integrate multimedia tools to the point where people become authors in the medium of their day.** When students are creating themselves, learning is taking place. **And teachers will be at the epicenter of this**."

● In many schools, students are already engaged in multimedia learning where they are acquiring **new knowledge and skills in the course of designing, planning and producing** a multimedia product. Students sharpen their **planning and organizational skills**, learn to **present information in compelling ways**, synthesize and analyze **complex content and data**, practice **research and technical skills** and learn how academic subject matter applies to **the real world.**

Why Should I Consider Multimedia?

Why should an already-busy music educator even think about including multimedia in his or her classroom repertoire?

● One of the **biggest threats** to our current programs is **what kids can do today without teachers.** With an electronic keyboard and computer, they can compose, perform, record, produce and share customized CDs. What **used to cost tens of thousands of dollars** can **now** be done with a **relatively inexpensive** keyboard and computer.

● As technology progresses, sound and sound design will play an **ever-more important role** in multimedia communication. If music (sound) educators do not step up and **take ownership of the learning opportunity**, others will.

● Multimedia learning will **attract** a new set of **students to your program.** Multimedia learning meets the needs of **students with an interest in music and a great interest in technology.**

Multimedia Learning. . .

● **enhances the learning experience** and **introduces the arts** to those who would not otherwise have the opportunity

TIP 21

- reinforces language arts and communication skills
- invigorates the teaching process
- addresses music education standards
- **facilitates interdisciplinary relationships** between the music department and other academic subjects
- **provides real-world applications** for students

Where Do I Start?

The advancement of arts-related technology is often perceived to be too rapid to assimilate, let alone grasp and articulate to today's student. Begin by asking yourself a **few simple questions:**

- **What are your interests and expertise? What do you bring** to improve student communication skills and enhance understanding of music (the science of sound)?

- **What hardware and software is available? Take an inventory:** film editing equipment, digital video cameras, projection equipment, sound equipment and computers. What does the school media center have available? Are there local computer loan programs? What do students have? (Check the age of the computers; **multimedia requires** ample memory and disk space.)

- **If you need hardware or software, consider** having it **donated**; asking your PTA, other **parent groups** or your **school council** for funds; contacting **local foundations**; **partnering with other departments** to write grants and share expensive equipment.

- **Think about your own requirements.** Are you a technology beginner, or do you need just a little technical help? Work with a **colleague**, take a **class**, attend a **conference**, use software **tutorials**, do a project yourself—**learn by doing. Students can be your greatest teachers!**

- **What do I need to teach?** Look at your curriculum. A multimedia project can **combine a number of skills and standards into one very motivating project.** Though the purpose of multimedia is communication, the purpose of the project is to provide a **rich learning experience** for students.

- **What is the project?** If you are trying a multimedia project for the first time, select a **topic you feel** comfortable with. A single class topic from which subgroups can select subtopics is a good place to start. Make sure there are opportunities for students to have **primary investigations.**

- **What multimedia project will the students create?** Involve the students in this decision! Examine your goals and objectives. Think about the forms of multimedia.

- **How much time will we spend on this?** Be realistic about the amount of time the project will take to complete. Think through the project thoroughly—and then build in extra time.

- **How will I involve students in the decision making?** Work with the students to list all of the decisions that need to be made between the day the project is started and when it is to be finished. **With the students' input, decide** which decisions are yours, which are theirs and which will be made together.

- **What resources will I need?** These depend on the project. Some **general categories to consider** are library materials, field trips, people as resources, the Internet, news media and original research.

- **How will I measure what students learn?** Remember to **plan ahead** for how to measure at least one key outcome the project is designed to accomplish. An important part of the assessment component is to **establish baseline data** before students begin working on the project.

- **What is the real-world connection?** How does the project **relate to the lives** of the students? Will the students' work be useful to others? Will the students see the connection between what they are doing and the real world?

Supporting Music Education:
Concert Thoughts

Too many excellent presentations are tainted by failure to **take care of the many details of a production.** We must take full advantage of the opportunities awaiting our students. The concert is our students' opportunity to show their parents or community audiences what they can do.

Pre-Concert: Calm or Chaos?

The most challenging part of a concert is the half-hour before the performance. How you manage that time is critical for a successful concert.

- **Students should know** where and when to report. They should also know what your procedural expectations are well ahead of concert day.

- **Be sure that concert requirements** regarding reporting times and locations, rehearsals and concert dress are shared with parents. This will require multiple methods of communication, including letters home, inclusion in school-wide newsletters, e-mails, postings on school Web sites, phone calls and countless announcements to students.

- **Arrange for the necessary help to address** all of the last-minute crises that are inevitable before each performance. Call on a colleague (or parent) for assistance and be sure to acknowledge and thank your helpers appropriately.

- **Rehearse in the performance space.**

- **Develop a concert production procedure or checklist** so everything will run smoothly. Include entering and exiting the stage, tuning, standing for bows, transitioning between selections as well as between the various performing ensembles.

Concert Length

- **At the elementary and middle school levels**, concerts should last no longer than one hour. If you cannot get through all of your ensembles in this time, consider having a second concert. Leave audiences wanting more so that they will return for future concerts.

- Although the ideal concert length is one hour, **high school programs often run 90 minutes** so that all ensembles may perform. As much as possible, give each group an equal amount of performance time so that one ensemble does not monopolize the program.

- **For school assemblies,** work with your colleagues to write out a minute-by-minute performance script and stick to it. Be sure to assign time for student movement and applause.

- When performing school assemblies, **plan an upbeat program** that is appropriate to the purpose of the assembly. Consider that students are performing for their peers and want to perform well for their friends.

TIP 22

- **This is your big opportunity** to impress your students and staff. Consider producing the concert with a different mix of material for the students during the day than you would for the parents in the evening.

Who is Running the Show?

- **Someone must "control" or "produce"** the presentation at all times. If your building administrator is not available throughout the performance to set the correct concert tone and ensure it will be maintained, you must:

- **Assume leadership of the situation.** You have the most to lose.

- **Discuss directly with the audience** your high expectations for their behavior.

- **Watch out for the transitions.** Someone needs to be assigned to cover as groups move about and set up for their performance. Have "sponge" activities planned to "sop up" the transitions. This can be done through student solos, announcements, echo clapping or sing-a-longs. These are excellent opportunities to mention links between music education and high student achievement. Inaction will usually default to boredom. Once you lose the audience, you seldom get them back.

- **Comment on and reinforce good behavior** at the conclusion of the program. Print audience expectations in the concert programs on a regular basis.

- **Give out public thanks** appropriately and acknowledge your school administration and school board for their support of the arts programs.

Concert Behavior

- Good concert behavior is learned and it is the music educator's job to teach audience etiquette. Good concert behavior **cannot be taken for granted.**

- Good concert behavior **needs to be taught** in all arts classes (classroom and performance).

- Good concert behavior **must be taught, reinforced, rewarded and re-taught.** This may be the only time in a student's life that this concept is addressed.

- **Remember: If not us, then who?**

- **Parents need as much direction** in the evening concerts as students do at the daytime assemblies. Since many parents do not know the proper responses, simply guide them along appropriately. (At the beginning of a multi-movement work, for example, you could simply explain that it is the practice in these types of pieces to hold the applause until after the final movement has been performed.)

- **Establish the proper concert atmosphere** through a short speech or concert program comments that can be used district-wide.

Programming Considerations

Your performance literature is your course of study.

- **Is it quality material** that serves as a good teaching tool?

- **Is it at the appropriate level of difficulty?** It is easy to justify music that is too easy. It is very difficult to justify a work that can never sound good because it is beyond the students' ability level. We all over-program, but do you make a habit of it?

- **Does your program have variety?** (Fast-slow, loud-soft, classic-contemporary, secular-sacred, languages, etc.) Have you included material for your students, your audience and yourself?

- **If you are sharing a concert,** how does your programming complement that of your colleagues?

- **Have you scheduled adequate rehearsal time with the accompanist** to ensure that you, the students and the accompanist are thoroughly prepared for a quality performance?

- **Do you include "informances" as part of your programming?** Taking a section of the concert to inform the audience about the process is a critical component of community arts education. This can be done through sight-reading a work, explaining with musical demonstration the musical development of a specific section or the rehearsal of a small section from a work to be featured in the next concert.

- **Have you asked your principal or a board member to give the Opening Remarks?** This provides an opportunity for one of your educational leaders to talk in front of a friendly audience.

- **Have you asked students to share what skills they have acquired in preparing for the concert?** Choose students to talk about what they have learned when introducing each selection. The audience will be pleasantly surprised at how much it really takes to perform well.

- **What is the perfect concert length?** The program where the audience leaves feeling that they would have liked to have heard one more number!

TIP 22

Production Considerations

Microphone Use

- Take the time to prevent possible sound problems.
- Have your students been instructed on how to use a microphone?
- Have they successfully practiced using a microphone?
- Are the levels set properly?
- Have you checked how they will sound from the back of the room?
- Have you asked someone else to listen to ensure quality control?
- Have you enlisted necessary assistance?

Technology

- Become totally familiar with the technology you are using—sound board, lighting board, tape recorders, CD players, computers, video recorders or projectors.
- Make arrangements to videotape the assembly or concert.
- Share the recordings with your students.
- Use the recordings for your personal assessment and growth.
- Know copyright regulations when recording concert material.

Program

This is another way to inform audience members about your school's music education program.

- The audience program must be visually appealing, neat and free of errors.
- Include your mission statement.
- Include advocacy information about the importance of arts education for students.
- Make sure someone is assigned to hand out programs and direct the audience to seating or restrooms.

Hands and Shoes; Attention to Festival P's and Q's

Courtesy of Marcia M. Neel, retired Supervisor of the Secondary Music Education Program of the Clark County School District, headquartered in Las Vegas, Nevada

Many of you have heard me talk about my "Hands and Shoes" philosophy. It has to do with attending to details—specifically with regard to musical performances, but also with regard to the many non-musical items which contribute to, or detract from, the performance. Festival is so much more than "performing the music." With this in mind, I would like to make several recommendations—a checklist, if you will—to use in preparing for your next performance. This list comes from items that have been observed at this year's festivals, so please keep a copy on your computer for next year so that you can review it with your students or even

place the appropriate sections in your student handbook. I still see Festival as a Formal Concert Event and ask that you treat it with that in mind.

1. Conductor Attire

Directors should wear appropriate attire when conducting. For formal festivals and concerts, women should wear a longer dress or skirt rather than something above or even at the knee. Formal pants are also appropriate. Men should wear a suit or tux. Accompanists should be dressed in black or in the same uniform as the performers. They should also wear black shoes. (Don't forget to wipe the dust off your shoes—it can be seen from the hall.) At the All-City and JV Festivals, directors may wear the same uniform—or a matching uniform—as the students. Basic black is always appropriate. Ladies should err on the side of conservatism.

2. Student Attire

Students should wear appropriate attire that provides a uniform appearance. This instills a sense of pride in their ensemble. Black pants require black socks and black shoes for performers. In many cases, students can get away with just wearing black socks if they forget to wear their black shoes. From the hall, you can't tell the difference. You can, however, tell if students are wearing white socks or black socks with athletic shoes. Some schools have purchased extra shoes to have available for students who need them. There is always a way to do this—visit with your supervisor if this is an economic issue at your school.

If possible, girls should wear either all pants or all skirts. Long black skirts can be purchased at a variety of locations at a variety of prices. Determine what works best for your situation but remember that uniformity is extremely important. Encourage your students to "hand down" their uniform as they progress into the next ensemble. You might want to visit with your administrator for financial assistance if needed for some students.

Hair should be worn off the face. This includes both students and conductors. Whether singing or playing, it is important that nothing get in the way. Students do not realize how many times they are pushing hair out of their faces with their hands or with a toss of the head. This is extremely distracting during performances. NO SUNGLASSES.

Students should wear their uniforms similarly. Take time to discuss with your students how to wear their uniform. T-shirts should be tucked in.

When wearing t-shirts or polo shirts, make a decision about the pants (for example: either all black, all jeans or all khaki). Decide whether the shirt should be buttoned all the way to the top or not. If boys are going to wear a t-shirt under the polo shirt, the t-shirt should be white.

TIP 22

It goes without saying that gum chewing, wearing sunglasses, chains and "nuisance items" are not appropriate. A uniform appearance (not to be confused with expensive uniforms) is expected and adjudicated at Festival.

3. Jewelry

Earrings and necklaces should not be seen unless they are part of the uniform. (Earrings that do not hang off the ears are appropriate and necklaces may be tucked in so long as they do not show.) Large jewelry pieces take away from the uniform look of the ensemble.

4. Audience Etiquette

This is considered to be a Formal Concert Setting and it is important that your students, and their parents, know what that means. Be sure to address audience etiquette ahead of time and often. If students know what the expectation is, they will behave appropriately. As you know, I reinforce this often at Festival. This past year, there were schools that received audience penalties in their scores because of such poor behavior. Please reinforce the fact that Festival is as much about learning how to be in the audience in a Formal Concert Setting as it is about the performance itself. The following is thus expected of students while they are listening to performances.

- Students should sit tall in their seats.
- Students should be quiet listeners and focus on exemplary elements of the performance.
- Students should remain seated during the entire performance.
- Flash photography should not occur during the performance. (Photos are permitted at the All-City and JV Festivals since these are considered to be entry-level events.)
- Cell phones should be turned off or put into the silent mode.

5. Applause

I find that students/audience members do not know about applause. Below, please find the expectation in a Formal Concert Setting. If you begin teaching this from the beginning of the year, students (and eventually parents) will know what to do by the time Festival occurs in the spring.

The audience should applaud for the first 8–10 performers who enter the stage and the same when they exit at the conclusion of the performance.

Applause should occur whenever someone is announced or recognized.

After each selection, applause should occur when the arms of the conductor have come all the way down to his or her side after the final cutoff. The selection is not over until this point.

6. Stage Etiquette

Be sure to address stage etiquette. The adjudication begins the moment the first student steps onto the stage. Discuss with them how to "take the stage." Once students are on the stage, they should not speak to one another unless absolutely necessary. Laughing on the stage is never appropriate.

Rehearse getting on and off the stage quietly, that is, where to go on the risers, when to stand/sit when the conductor enters, etc. All of this is part of the performance experience.

7. Performance Etiquette

The performance evaluation begins the moment the first student steps onto the stage, rather than when the first note is played, so please ensure that your students understand this. They are to enter the stage; go directly to their location; then demonstrate proper instrument rest position. STUDENTS ARE NOT TO CARRY ON CONVERSATIONS DURING THIS TIME.

Conductors should turn around and acknowledge the audience when they applaud for the ensemble's performance. Students should be taught to look at the audience and smile during the applause. Do NOT allow them to turn to the next selection during this time. There is nothing worse than applauding for an ensemble whose members are turning to the next piece during this time. Students should bring up the next selection only after the director has turned back to face the ensemble. In jazz band, soloists should definitely acknowledge applause with a smile or nod when the audience applauds for the solo.

THE BIG PICTURE: ATTENDING TO MUSICAL DETAILS

Be sure that you are teaching musical skills through the music itself rather than just teaching musical selections. This is why music is our textbook. In the past, too many ensembles have "performed notes" without attending to the "how to" of singing or playing. If you need ideas on how to teach good tone, for example, ask for pedagogical assistance. There are many resident experts who are happy to help. If you are not sure what music might be appropriate for your ensemble, ask. Don't settle for a "good" performance. Debbie Brockett, principal of Silvestri MS, was awarded the NMEA Administrator of the Year Award and in her acceptance speech, she said, "Good is the enemy of great." Each day, students must grow in some facet, and it is up to us to never compromise on our expectations.

Want more tips on keeping music strong in your schools?
Visit the site devoted to all things music advocacy: **www.supportmusic.com**

TIP 22

Supporting Music Education:
Audience Guidelines

Becoming a discerning, supportive and knowledgeable audience member is an important part of a student's education. Successful audience participation requires skill, discretion, common sense, discipline and a bit of knowledge.

You have worked very hard to prepare your students to perform in concert. One final step remains: It is also essential that you set a high expectation for audience behavior and appropriate participation.

- Most of us learn to be "an audience" in front of the television or at the movies. This is quite different from actually being present in a room with other people—most likely, people you don't know and who don't know you—at a live performance. At live performances, **we enter into relationships**, both with the performers and with our fellow audience members.

- **One of the pleasures of live performance** is spontaneity, but what is required of an audience is spontaneity within certain discreet boundaries.

- **Appropriate performance behaviors change** according to the type of performance we are attending. When we comment on a performance, we are not only voicing our opinions, but also revealing our knowledge—or lack of knowledge.

Choose from the appropriate event information below and consider including it in your program.

At Live Performances

- **Be amazed, impressed, challenged, fascinated and appreciative.**

- **Applaud** when the performers walk onstage and at the end of the piece—but not in the middle. Look at the printed program: Some pieces consist of several "movements." It is customary to wait in silence between these movements and then to applaud at the end of the entire piece.

- **Refrain from talking during the performance.** The performers and our fellow audience members are trying to concentrate. The medium is sound, and unwanted sound competes with the performance.

- **Show appreciation through applause.** Cheering is not appropriate at a live concert.

- **Refrain from taking flash photos or making video or audio recordings.** Flash photos disrupt the performers, and copyright laws prohibit recordings of any sort.

TIP 23

In Addition, at a Jazz Concert

- **Get excited!**
- **Applaud** a solo that you find particularly great. You may show appreciation in the middle of a piece.
- **Express** yourself more openly than at a classical concert, but remember that cheering is still not appropriate.

In Addition, at a Dance Concert

- **Be amazed and fascinated with the movement of the human body.**
- **Applaud** anywhere in the midst of the dance. You may applaud a particularly difficult or well-executed move, step or leap.

At a Visual Arts Event

- **Examine, ogle, question, speak with the artist, scrutinize, be baffled, converse, melt, raise your eyebrows—but also show respect for the creative process.**
- **Refrain from touching** unless specifically asked.
- **You may ask permission from the artist to take photographs.**

At the Theatre

- **Be fascinated, cry, laugh, get angry and smile.**
- **Applaud** at the end of a scene, act, speech or zinger. In other words, you may respond in the middle of the piece.
- **Refrain from talking and taking flash photos or making recordings.**

- Don't distract the performers before, during or after the performance.

At a Poetry or Fiction Reading

- **Listen in silence.** Cultivate the ability to let the words play on your imagination. Let the voice of the reader and his or her language conjure up images in your mind's eye.
- If a poet is reading more than one poem, he or she will tell you this at the beginning of the reading. **Do not applaud until** all of the poems have been read.

And Finally

- Standing **ovations are rare in the real world**. Be judicious with your standing ovations. They should not become so commonplace that performers who receive only warm applause fear that the audience disapproves of their performance.

Informances

- **Informances** (opportunities where the audience gains information about an arts discipline while at a performance) are extremely effective advocacy tools. Informances can be one number in a program or an entire production.
- **Build opportunities for the audience to actively participate** (sing, move, emulate, play, etc.) in them.
- **Encourage the audience to look at the process** of creating, not just the product. It is through "process" that students become enriched through the arts.

Want more tips for keeping music strong in your schools?
Visit the site devoted to all things music advocacy: **www.supportmusic.com**

TIP 23

Tips for Success is produced by the Music Achievement Council • www.musicachievementcouncil.org • 800.767.6266

Supporting Music Education:
Choose to Teach

How do you know if you want to become a music teacher? Some students just know and others make that decision when considering career options. For many students, sharing the joy of music becomes their passion.

The information that follows will assist you and your students in **making an informed choice**. Becoming a music teacher can be an **extremely rewarding and challenging career**. If you **love to make music and enjoy working with others**, there is no better way to **convey that passion** than by sharing **your knowledge and enthusiasm** as a professional music educator.

What Does a Music Teacher Do?

- **teach** classes
- **share** their love of music with students and other teachers
- **prepare** lesson plans
- **develop** curriculum
- **assess** and **evaluate** student progress
- **share** student progress with parents, fellow teachers and school administrators
- **prepare** and **perform** concerts
- **develop** course content based on local, state and national content standards
- **ensure** success for all students while respecting their various interests, abilities and cultural backgrounds
- **use** motivation and positive reinforcement as effective classroom-management tools
- **model** professionalism in all aspects of the profession
- **demonstrate** ultimate responsibility for resources, including:
    - time
    - money
    - facilities
    - equipment
    - transportation
    - people
- **communicate** with all parties on a regular basis
- **lead** with enthusiasm

What Do I Have to Know to Be Able to Teach Music?

- **Understand pedagogy**: The techniques of teaching choral, instrumental and classroom music at all levels—elementary school, middle school and high school

- **Demonstrate** an accomplished level of **musicianship**: Mastery of your instrument, conducting, sight reading, singing and studying a score

- **Develop effective time management, organization**, communication and facilitation skills

- **Advocate for music education**: Learn why music is important for all children and how being involved with music contributes to brain development of young children and enhanced student achievement

- **Show compassion**: A music educator must be exceedingly sensitive to all student needs

- **Maintain high expectations**: Focus on achievement and motivate students to meet established goals successfully

What Can I Do Now to Gain Experience Necessary for Teaching?

- **Teach** private lessons on your primary instrument
- **Volunteer** to tutor students
- **Work** at a band camp or summer program
- **Observe and assist** a teacher who can help you gain experience and confidence
- **Join** the future teachers club
- **Demonstrate leadership** in everything you do

Does the Music Education Program Focus on Both Process and Performance?

The process of making music—preparing the product—is very important. Much of the value of music is **experiencing the process** of getting the performance ready. It is through this pedagogical focus that students learn and develop critical thinking skills.

Does the Music Education Program Provide a Variety of Experiences Observing and Working with Students?

A quality collegiate Music Education curriculum should prepare you

- to teach music in any setting through relevant coursework and classroom experiences addressing how all children, adolescents and young adults learn and develop in music

- to develop and implement age-appropriate teaching strategies through the use of appropriate materials

- for hands-on classroom experiences long before the final semester of the senior year

- to pass all competency exams (music and others) that may be required for certification/licensure

What Does Certification/Licensure Mean?

Eye on Education (WGBH and PBS) defines **Teacher Certification** as "a process by which teachers become recognized by the state as expert teachers, implying that a teacher has mastered the complex art of teaching." **Teacher Licensure** is defined as "the process by which teachers receive permission from the state to teach. States have minimum requirements, such as the completion of certain coursework and experience as a student teacher. Some states, faced with shortages of teachers in particular areas, grant teachers emergency licenses and allow them to take required courses while they are full-time teachers."

In completing a degree in music education, you have completed the specific requirements of a degree-granting institution; this will provide you with "entry level" skills for a teaching position. As such, states will issue either a certificate or a license, which will enable a new educator to teach in a public school setting. (Many private institutions do not require the same types of teaching credentials.) If you teach in a different state than the one in which you were trained, you may receive a temporary license until you meet the requirements of that specific state.

Certificates/Licenses are required to be renewed periodically, so you will want to contact the State Department of Education in all of the states in which you plan to apply for a teaching position. **State licensing procedures vary,** but most require ongoing professional development, so it is important to start early by accruing post-graduate credits.

What is the Range of Certification/ Licensure Options?

- Each state sets its own criteria for certification/licensing, a process that **acknowledges the preparation** received from an accredited college or university. In addition to possessing the appropriate college degree, most states require teacher candidates to provide proof of passing

TIP 24

Tips for Success is produced by the Music Achievement Council • www.musicachievementcouncil.org • 800.767.6266

scores on examinations designed to test knowledge in a variety of subjects. Some states allow time for teachers to prepare to take these exams, but many do not. *Most universities provide access to a number of these tests so that students may take them while still matriculated.*

- **Reciprocal certification agreements** also exist between many states, making it possible for teachers who are certified in one state to relocate to another.

- Many music education programs are designed to prepare music teachers for more specific areas of concentration, such as choral, classroom and instrumental music, or K–12.

What are the Requirements for Acceptance into the Music Education Program?

In addition to their own established criteria for admission, most teacher education programs generally require all or a variety of the following:

- a specified grade-point average (GPA)

- an audition

- a pre-professional skills test, such as an ear-training or theory test

- an essay

- an interview

- a portfolio, which should serve as a reflection of your high school music career, including copies of:

  - concert programs

  - awards, certificates

  - letters of reference

  - appropriate photos, DVDs, CDs

  - festival (solo and ensemble) ratings

  - indicators of leadership at school, church, community

  - list of memberships in clubs and other organizations; offices/positions held

What about a Placement File/Portfolio?

Many universities provide **Job Placement Offices** on their campuses and offer assistance in career planning through the establishment of a Placement File/Portfolio for each teacher candidate. This tool should be thought of as your promotional package, so spend extra time to make sure

it reflects what you want prospective employers to see. It should be neat, well-organized, provide evidence of good communication skills (including written skills) and show experience working with a diverse student population.

The Placement File/Portfolio should consist of a Résumé that includes:

- Teaching philosophy

- Degree(s) held

- University attended

- Job/Related work experience (list chronologically with most recent year first; remember to include student teaching as well as related summer experiences— particularly those with a music emphasis)

- Membership in professional associations, organizations, clubs, activities; offices/positions held (include attendance at conferences)

- Honors and awards

- Names of prior supervisors, references (include complete contact information)

- Sample lesson plans used in student teaching that demonstrate successful experience working with students of diverse learning styles and including

- Content standard(s) being addressed

- Clearly stated, measurable objectives

- Materials needed

- Prior knowledge and experiences required

- Teaching strategies to be used to meet the objectives

- Indicators of success

- Recommendations for follow-up

- Other **written** materials used in student teaching, which could include

- Sample course expectations

- Letters to parents

- Concert programs

- Student motivators

- Transcripts

- Letters of recommendation (3) from any or all of the following:

  - Cooperating teacher(s)

- School administrator(s)
- University supervisor
- Private teacher(s)/other professional(s) who can attest to your teaching expertise
- Parent(s) of students
- Proof of degree
- Test results (scores) for teacher proficiency exams, if available
- Optional: Awards, certificates
- Optional: Appropriate photos, DVDs, CDs

Many school districts want to watch prospective teachers demonstrate their skills by teaching a lesson at one of the schools. Teacher candidates should be prepared for this situation in case it is a required part of the application process.

What are the Alternatives to Teaching in the Public Schools?

- Parochial schools
- Private magnate schools
- Charter schools
- Symphony schools or outreach programs
- Private instruction

Will I Have to Give Up Performing to Teach Music?

No! There are many opportunities throughout communities of all sizes to continue performing. **Performing is an essential tool** of any good music educator and provides an opportunity to be a good role model for your students.

Want more tips on keeping music strong in your schools?
Visit the site devoted to all things music advocacy: **www.supportmusic.com**

Tips for Success is produced by the Music Achievement Council • www.musicachievementcouncil.org • 800.767.6266